Allitera Verlag

REGINA MEHLER leads the marketing team for central Europe at Adobe and is responsible for developing their marketing strategy. With over 20 years of experience in the IT industry, her passion is for branding, innovation and ROI oriented marketing projects, as well as the integration of marketing and sales.

Before beginning at Adobe, she was responsible for 15 countries in her role as Marketing Director for Central/Eastern Europe and Russia and Siebel Systems, and then led the worldwide marketing at Software AG in Darmstadt, Germany as their Vice President of Corporate Marketing Strategy. In 2008, her work rebranding Software AG was recognized with the Gold European Corporate Design Award. In 2009, she received e.g. the American ReBrand Award and in 2010, she founded the Women Speaker Foundation.
Visit her website www.regina-mehler.com

Regina Mehler

The Phoenix Effect

Thinking outside of the box: Innovational Management and Marketing

Allitera Verlag

More information about the publishing house:
www.allitera.de

February 2013
Allitera Verlag
An imprint of Buch&media GmbH, Munich
© 2013 Buch&media GmbH, Munich
Cover design: Kay Fretwurst, Freienbrink
Printed in Germany · ISBN 978-3-86906-314-0

Table of Contents

Prologue 9

Creatively Constructive: 1,000 Ideas in One Day!:
The way to successful, innovative marketing 13

If you want to be innovative, you are going to need ideas. Ideally, you need many so that you can quickly choose the best from them. You can achieve this perfection, if you practice the right creative techniques and make sure you have an innovative culture in your company and environment.

"WHAT TO DO AND WHAT TO LET OTHERS DO"
BY ANKE MEYER-GRASHORN 24

Idea-deliverers and Inspiration-givers:
How a Good Network Inspires You Professionally and Privately ... 31

"IMPORTANT PEOPLE HAVE IMPORTANT CONTACTS"
BY MONIKA SCHEDDIN 44

Cooperation with Other Companies:
The Advantage of Business Partnerships 50

Two are often better than one. The same goes in the business world. Therefore, it is excellent when two companies get together and form a partnership. This chapter informs you about the different types of partnerships and different ways to build them.

"TAKING ON THE FULL RISK – FOR ONLY HALF OF THE SUCCESS?"
BY GABRIELE RITTINGHAUS 62

Selecting Employees and Motivation: Creating the Ideal Team 66

An innovative manager needs a team who is also focused on innovation. In order to do this, he needs to find the appropriate candidates and motivate the crew responsible for developing new ideas. This works best with a business relationship that is based on respect, fairness, and trust. This chapter describes in detail how you can get there.

"Diversity of Innovative Factors"
By Torsten Bittlingmaier 80

Mutual Goals, Mutual Success
Alignment: the Ideal Cooperation Between Marketing and Sales .. 88

If marketing wants to be innovative by themselves, they won't get very far, for marketing needs information from sales. It is therefore optimal when marketing and sales cooperate from the very first step in the planning process. This chapter shows you where the hurdles are and how to overcome them.

"Full Speed Ahead to Real Success"
By Sonja Sulzmaier 97

Beating your Own Drum:
How You Can Capitalize on Your Work 107

The more innovative an idea is, the more important it is to sell this idea. This requires constant effort and targeted self-marketing, that gives the idea the correct positing, without being too pushy. This also requires the preparation of a clever presentation. This chapter details how to do this successfully.

"Fire and Flame for Innovation"
By Guido Happe 117

The Numbers Have to be There:
Here's How Your Marketing Can be Measurably More Effective ...   122

Nowadays, success must be measurable. In marketing, the Key Performance Indicators were always the way to measure success. Currently, executives and even your colleagues do not just want to see the costs, but also the numbers relating to successes. The chapter lists the possibilities of measuring success.

"NOTHING IS CREATED THROUGH PURE THINKING"
BY NEIL MORGAN   126

About the Guest Authors of the Passages   133

Prologue

Imagine this: You are Steve Jobs and your company is failing (much like Apple in the 90's). You need to revive your enterprise – so what do you do? Simple. You revolutionize digital communication. You make sure that information and music are always available – everywhere. You produce the iPod, then the iPhone, and finally you introduce the iPad to the market. But above everything, you reinforce an innovative culture within your company. You successfully create an environment where employees in different departments are able to test and develop their new ideas.

This is a dream for someone like me. I am often curious, but I am easily bored when there is too much routine at work. As a marketing director, that is why I motivate my team to frequently push the limits of their creativity. With trainings, moderated workshops, and in-house presentations of all different themes we motivate and inspire ourselves to think outside of the box.

I am convinced that you can learn to think creatively just like one would learn a language – by taking the time to practice often. Time is one of the key factors for innovation. For example, at the company 3M, it is explicitly stated that employees should invest fifteen percent of their time at work in their own projects. Keep in mind that in a forty hour work week this can amount to 6 hours of time. The success is evident in the company, for it was the employees of 3M that invented Post-it notes. Nowadays, Post-its are an irreplaceable part of any office desk.

As a marketing manager for software corporations, my personal strength regarding innovation lies in the ability to bring extraordinary projects to life, for example, the IT Vision Tour, a journey for the leaders of the biggest European IT companies to meet Bill Gates (for more on this, see page 58). This was a project that I developed with my team and various partner companies, proving all the skeptics wrong ("Impossible!") because we made the unthinkable doable. We were able to make contacts and deepening relationships that wouldn't be possible with classic marketing techniques (at least not in the short period of time that we had).

My newest project is the Women Speaker Foundation that I founded together with a PR expert from my network. This foundation supports women who have something to say and helps them prepare to be on stage. The women are very well-versed but they trust themselves less than their male colleagues. This is what we would like to change, and the innovative Women Speaker Foundation can provide the platform.

Because routine means the end of innovation, I consciously take time off to concentrate on innovative projects. I also frequently prescribe time for my coworkers to develop creativity and new ideas by attending workshops and presentations, as well as visiting networking events (and these events are not just designated for the marketing sector, but also various other areas). Whether one is a bookkeeper or a builder, a teacher or a technician, conversations with people from other industries lead to the development of new ideas. I am not only a convinced networker myself, I also set aside a budget to finance my team members in the activities listed above.

In addition to time and inspiration, the wiliness to take risks is a key factor of innovation. The correlation between opportunity and risk is recognized in the area of capital investments. Generally, the higher the risk, the higher the return. This is also true for innovation. A new product idea can be a great hit or a flop, but no one is able to tell you this in advance. Management must be ready to make key decisions to implement an idea, but they must face the fact that money invested in a vision can also be wasted and completely lost.

One cannot predict the outcome of decisions regarding innovation. Different scenarios and probability of their outcomes are calculable, but, in the end, a decision should be based on your gut feeling and determination rather than the solid prognosis. Guido Happe, an innovation consultant, calls this process "deciding before experiencing". A circumstance that happens all too often is that one avoids innovational ideas and instead chooses to focus on predictable numbers and shareholder value. With innovational ideas, things can always go wrong, and then the heads will roll. No wonder there is no comfort in being innovative.

Companies that want to be innovative have to increase their tolerance of mistakes, and, with that, send the right signals. The employees must know that their company is prepared to deal with flops and mistakes, then true innovation can be experienced. This has nothing to do with recklessness, but rather the opposite. I must know exactly which risks I am able to take and how I will react to the worst case scenario. Only then would I advocate for the project.

Innovation is like pioneering. In the past, there were crazy people who sailed the oceans alone and fought through undiscovered territories. Today in the globalized world, a pioneer still has an unconventional character, but he must agree, convince, and communicate with others. Instead of sailing alone, he has to bring the others on board with him. "Alignment" is the name of the game. This term comes from biology and describes organisms in masses, which imitate the behavior of their neighbor. This is how a school of fish can quickly coordinate their movement together and protect themselves against predators (more on this topic on page 109).

Alignment is a characteristic of someone who wishes to be an innovative mastermind, because only together with the rest of his company can one reach his goals. The research and development department of a software company must know what the customer wants, what satisfies them, and what makes them unsatisfied. Bill Gates writes, "The unsatisfied customers are my favorite. They tell me exactly what I have to do better." Developers also need feedback from the sales teams because they are in direct contact with the customers. Then marketing must work directly with the sales team and customer when they want to develop campaigns that reach the heart of the customer.

The coworkers who hold such preconceptions like "The guys in research and development don't know..." or "Marketing has no idea..." or "Sales people are just..." need to substitute their prejudices with more open communication with each other. Mutual recognition of one another's competence, effective meetings with the exchange of know-how, as well as a fair and substantial exploration of new concepts should be on the agenda every day.

In the seven chapters of this book, I have systematically outlined how you can create a business culture where new concepts can be developed and achieved. You will find testimonials, to-do lists, and commentary in each chapter from specialists which will enhance my insight. Among the many who contributed to the book are Innovation Consultant, Guido Happe, Networking Specialist, Monika Scheddin, and Innovation Coach, Anke Meyer-Grashorn.

This book was also an innovation project for me; many of the factors described in this book played a part in its success. For example, I discovered the correct publisher and journalist who would support me in the writing of this book through recommendations of those in my network. I also met the experts who contributed valuable information through my network and only through the discussions with the publisher and my editorial sparring partner could I truly make this book a reality. In fact, as a testament to the power of networking, the title of this book arose in an email with my inner circle.

While writing, I was constantly leaving my desk because a change of place inspires me and brings me new ideas. So I am thankful that, while writing, I was able to travel a lot. San Francisco, Naples, Paris, Copenhagen, and the Alps are just a few of the points of origin for this book. The regular trips I took from Munich to the mountains helped me to overcome my writer's block. Even more important than the opportunity to change your perspective is your passion to do so. Writing this book was pure fun for me, simply due to the fact that I was able to master the additional work on the evenings and weekends (with a lot of understanding from my partner). An important aspect of every innovation project is that you should never lose sight of your goals. Only when a task is enjoyable will you be in a position to give it your all, overcome opposition, solve problems, and inspire others. You should always ask yourself, "What evokes your passion?"

With all of this (support, motivation and an array of business and private travels), I was able to create something that I couldn't have imagined one year ago. A book that perhaps can inspire you to new doings and successes, much like the Phoenix: the bird from Greek mythology that burns in the morning sun and arises from the ashes in a more rejuvenated form. That's how I see this project: developing something new and exciting from nothing and watching it succeed.

I look forward to your success stories and your opinion of this book at the following web address:
   www.regina-mehler.de

All the best,
Regina Mehler

Creatively Constructive: 1000 Ideas in One Day!

The way to successful, innovative marketing.

"Grab attention – at any cost!" That should be the motto of successful marketing, but with mailings, events, and other traditional marketing instruments, that's not always possible. If you want to demand the full attention of your clients, you have to have an exciting and stimulating plan to support your task. To do this, you really don't need a large budget (something that most marketers don't have anymore, since the financial crisis in 2009), but you do need good ideas – and preferably a continuous flow of them.

How does one create a creative atmosphere in which good ideas don't just thrive, but are also continuously produced systematically? One requirement would be curious, open-minded, and discussion-friendly thinkers. In other words: A team that believes that the imaginable is do-able. You need a circle of innovators who work openly and constructively together and (most importantly) are persevering – because there are necessary costs until the ultimate approach is developed.

It is always important to constantly have the market and current developments in your perspective. Companies who are unable to properly recognize these factors can lose more than just their connection to the market if their approach is outdated. Take, for example, the department store Quelle, who, among other things, were unable to successfully navigate themselves through the rising e-commerce business. While Amazon was booming, the traditional department store declared bankruptcy.

Whether in product development, customer service, or marketing departments, innovative ideas must be orientated on the current market and should be executed in a timely matter. Several companies have mastered excellence in innovation in the decades before, namely the Swedish furniture empire of Ikea. Their realm continues to grow and grow, all thanks to their good ideas. For example, the idea to lend a name to each product. The result: the furniture has become our friends, with whom we've (more or less) bonded in our home life.

Such marketing ideas are indeed big steps, requiring little money. Whoever would like to develop ideas needs, above all, methods and systems, in addition to a creative atmosphere and a good team. And these (here comes the pleasant news) are cultivated within the team.

> Seven Tips for the Development of Innovative Ideas
> - Trust yourself – it pays off
> - Think outside of the box
> - Develop and nurture creative methods
> - Be concrete: allow yourself to explore all ideas until the very end
> - Surround yourself with other innovators
> - Don't be afraid to take risks
> - Encourage the innovative ideas of others

Trim the Fat!

The years of excess can make you too comfortable – this is true for people and companies (who are made and managed by people). But, for man and business alike, there was a rude awakening when Lehman Bank crashed in America and the international economy plummeted into a worldwide financial crisis. Most companies reacted to the shock by drastically cutting the budgets of all departments, especially in marketing.

Of course, the goals remained the same. In short, the urgency increased while the means did not. For most marketing teams, that meant that we had to be quicker, better, and more creative. For the latter, we had to fetch outside support. Anke-Meyer Grashorn, creative expert, instructed us in the systematic development of creative ideas. With restricted phone and email capabilities, we traveled to a two-day retreat in Chiemsee, Germany and learned new creative methods to ripen innovative ideas – by the thousands!

Warming-Up for Beginners

"Just like the production of cars relies on a constant process of evolving ideas," says Anke-Meyer Grashorn, "one requirement is that everyone welcomes hard work." We were ready to tackle the hard work and began with the obligatory warm-up. Divided into groups, we were faced with the task of creating an image of a city in 2100 and presenting our ideas in the form of a collage. To do this, we were given a mountain of old newspapers and two hours' time. We discussed city names, potential advancements, and communication methods. We asked ourselves how the people would live and dress, what they would eat and what they would produce.

After a half an hour of intense discussion, even the more reserved colleague participated. They contributed funny, imaginative, out-of-this-world ideas. Suddenly, we had conceptualized Utopia: populated by creatures that possessed human characteristics, but looked like a unicellular organism. These creatures placed a huge amount of importance on environmental protection, due to the fact that they had developed a Beamer-like transportation system and had abolished the traditional methods of travel. The Utopians were coldblooded, and therefore didn't need to heat their houses. These ideas sprang forth simply because we had awakened our creativity.

The warm-up phase was complete.

From Cold Compresses to Premium Clients in the Icehotel

After everyone warmed up their brain, it was time for the second phase of the workshop. While brainstorming, we searched for sudden inspiration. Anything that popped into your head was allowed. Rating or evaluating even just one of these ideas was forbidden. Collecting our ideas was our first and foremost priority.

In this phase, we learned that most ideas are suffocated due to killer-phrases. These phrases are hidden in the heads of most people and they block their brain storming. "

"That doesn't work…" "We tried that before and it didn't work…" "That may work for others but not for us." "You need a really big budget to pull that off…"

Negative sentences like this are based on caution and risk prevention and block our creative thinking ability, explained Ms. Grashorn. With the help of the very simple, yet effective method of changing your perspective, we can learn to shut out these killer-phases and develop ideas with a more open mind.

Our keyword was cold compress. We searched for all kinds of associations with this word and casually came up with the following pretty quickly: fever, sickness, winter, skiing, Christmas, gingerbread, spices, India, Sari, Hindu, cows, fields – the ideas galloped through our heads and suddenly a substantial mind map had developed. Then, we had to change perspectives by replacing the word "cold compress" with the word "marketing", and this new term had to be related to the previous thoughts in our brainstorming session. As the word "winter" was moved to the center of our deliberations, we realized the urgency to react to the seasonality of the market, and therefore came up with the idea to hold seasonal campaigns – complete with relevant giveaways and incentives. For example, whoever recommended a client in the winter months received the seasonal gift of a scarf, a hat, or (depending on the volume of recommendations) a night in the Ice Hotel. We wanted to invite premium clients to a winter camp, in order to discuss product innovations with them. In short, the idea machine was up and running.

All in all, we were able to think outside of the box easier with our change in perspectives – and new insights and opinions were generated like never before.

Cultivating the tender flower of Creativity

After two days of hard, creative work at Chiemsee, we pursued many new ways of thinking and learned quite a few things. We also understood that this was only the beginning for us and that we had not yet reached our goal. For me, personally, this meant that I had to bottle my impatience. Like most managers these days, I appreciate when things advance quickly. In the end, we are all slaves to the quarter-end numbers and carved from quick success. However, the ability to methodically work together, creatively, in a team still has to grow. In our everyday life, we will have to envision the different procedures that we learned in the workshop and effectively work them into our efforts to go against our old pattern of thinking. For one whole year, we busied ourselves with the theme of creativity and integrating it into our daily routine until the seed of creativity was strong enough to withstand the pressure of our work at hand.

Fighting Software Pirates with Comic Characters

We don't train ourselves on the job for success day-by-day. For that, we turned to our Creative Expert for help. About five months after our experience at Chiemsee, we met again for a workshop in Prague. We started the meeting with our best practices. Every regional team presented their most important success story. It wasn't the most original approach, but it produced a really good atmosphere for exchanging information in the group. Asking oneself "What did we do well?" really set the tone for a positive status quo and emphasized the efficiency of the individual teams, as well as motivated the others to create both replications and new ideas. One of our success stories was a long-term anti-piracy campaign that we wanted to apply to the illegal software problem in Africa. The basic approach was playful: a computer game that was specifically developed for target groups and engaged different local partners in the campaign. The partners could even promote the game on their local websites. That's how we succeeded – by connecting the partners strongly to us so that we could use their contacts and influence to magnify the impact of the game. The beauty of this concept: we developed this once and executed it many times by translating the campaign into other languages and using it in other countries.

The second part of the workshop consisted of a rally through Prague that didn't just require knowledge, but also offensive communication skills. Our team was supposed to ask pedestrians if they were familiar with our company. It was a very interesting experience for the marketers, who rely heavily on market research but very rarely grapple with its preparation and development. To receive direct feedback on the street like that was a completely new feeling. The result? After the rally, our group was a real team, forged together by similar experiences, in a good mood and very motivated for the final creative tasks.

After the second workshop, I realized that I suddenly had the team that I wished for and with whom I could achieve what was expected of me: innovative marketing. The course was set. From there on, I was tasked with continuously injecting energy into the creative process, to make the new even newer and to, day-by-day, be the most creative (in the true sense of the word.)

Explicitly Allowed: Mistakes and Flops

Innovation requires not just a systematic creative process, but also proper business culture that embraces mistakes. Unfortunately, it's most often the case that businesses don't want to make any mistakes – and employees don't either. Of course, they then behave inconspicuously, going after the motto that if they don't do anything wrong, they may advance to the next level.

Businesses that want to transform must be prepared to take risks. They must believe that one learns from their mistakes and therefore becomes more intelligent, rather than the opposite. More importantly, the company should communicate this idea. Only then do the employees recognize that their managers stand behind successful, innovative campaigns, as well as the unsuccessful ones.

By the same token, employees will continuously choose the way with the least opposition, should they fail at an innovative project, as they are in fear for their jobs.

Most important for a company poised for innovation: Whoever risks everything must have everything within their scope, above all their employees. For my team members that means they must follow the golden rule: Tell me when there is risk so that I may deal with it. As their manager, I can then prepare for the worst case scenario. However I would like to know the risks up front, since I am the one responsible for any uncertainty in the end.

Do you read...

The more intensively that you care for your culture of innovation, the better it functions. Therefore, we have methods to advance creativity (in addition to our workshops.) For example, we regularly invite different experts into our company. They lecture us on the new movements in trends, the changes in the media world, the web 2.0, and they introduce the newest e-Marketing tools. Our so-called "marketing lectures", which were originally planned to be exclusively for our marketing colleagues, suddenly generated interest from other departments. At this point, we've also extended invitations to members of the press, partners, and clients – and they are always in attendance. For everyone who can't make it, we offer the lectures as web seminars and record them as podcasts that can be downloaded at a later time.

I also deliberately cultivate creativity in private settings and am constantly searching for new inspiration. In accordance with the motto that "anything different is good", I purposely look for opportunities to keep my spirit awake and open. My network is really helpful for this because I try to keep in contact with numerous people who work in completely different industries.

But it's not just my network that inspires me. When I am looking for a good slogan, I buy a variety of newspapers. From car magazines to interior decorating journals, their bold tones motivate me to develop new ideas. Talking with friends in cafes or with colleagues at the airport also gives me impulses. I can find inspiration anywhere I can speak with friends or observe others. Where do you live? What do you do? Are you in a rut? Or are you innovative? How would you evaluate my latest work issue? And when I think about my friend (who is a hospital nurse in the intensive unit) and how she would find my latest work dilemma to be insignificant, it soothes my mind wherever I am. This, in turn, makes it easier for me to reassess and finally reach a solution.

Making Time for Innovation

Effectiveness through innovation consequentially means creating thinking and work time for the innovation process. New paths can only be carved when there is enough space for them. A marketing manager who relies obstinately on his calendar is like a hamster in a wheel: he will not be an innovator. The key is this: break free from your routine! A good marketing manager cannot be the caretaker of archaic and redundant processes. The cost is too high. If businesses are prepared to pay the going rate for a marketing manager, then they are allowed to have higher expectations. Therefore, offer them more. Offer them your innovation.

The success of an innovation-provider is decisive upon their ability to be organized and plan time for their innovational projects. Successful is he who is able to bring the team, the business, and the plan together in harmony.

Therefore, as a marketing manager, you should use all of your time management tools and tricks to keep some time free for innovation. Easier said than done. Even if you are a motivated and dynamic person, you can often fall into the deadly trap of convenience and routine. Don't allow this to happen, because an old friend of tediousness is a false feeling of security. Whoever knows a project's course also knows the main players, and can execute without any surprises, as if one had all the time in the world. It might be a little drab, but it's comfortable. A marketing manager should refrain from this. Your first task should always be to constantly look for something new, but without reinventing the wheel at the same time.

Because routine is real innovation-killer, every manager who wants to be innovative should deliberate how they will take care of the reoccurring everyday tasks while devoting time to his main goal: innovation. Only then can he concentrate on the major themes that really make a difference. I therefore recommend marketing organizations to give the classic marketing tasks to agencies or freelancers, so that the core team has spare time to donate to innovational projects.

After all, outsourcing the routine projects externally is a change in itself. Too much routine leads to symptoms of fatigue in external people as well. Only when responsibilities are altered after a certain period of time can one really fight against the rut that leads to boredom, neglectfulness, and lack of enthusiasm.

> **Seven Tips for a Creative Atmosphere**
>
> - Clean out your brain! Only then are you able to look outside of the box. As a manager, it is your responsibility to give your employees the necessary space they need.
> - Get out of the office. Try to get your coworkers to be more creative by taking a walk or going to the cafeteria alone or together in a group.
> - Collect suggestions from outside! Find out what other people are doing in different departments. Bring in external speakers.
> - Mistakes are allowed! Being afraid of failure blocks creativity and suffocates every new idea at its core. Be careful, you should make the same mistake only once and learn from it.
> - Employ workers from other industries. They will automatically bring a new perspective to things.
> - As a manager, set a good example! You do not have to be the creative one, but show how one brings in inspiration and implements it.
> - Support your coworkers to be active in networking. Amicable and friendly exchanges are essential.

> **How to Enhance your own Creativity**
>
> - Leave the workplace! Even a little walk can do remarkable things.
> - Do not become the lone wolf. Exchange your ideas with others and get their opinion on your problem areas.

- Create a heterogeneous network. Pursue new contacts, specifically in different industries. Very often, you will get exciting and innovative inspiration which you can apply to your environment (more about this in Chapter 2).
- Experience the creative methodology. It is possible to create new ideas continuously.
- Be informed and interested – you can find inspiration everywhere, whether at the newsstand, supermarket, or the opera ...
- Pay attention to down time. You need time to decompress. Then, you will suddenly experience new ideas out of nowhere.
- Develop your inner circle. Create small groups of good contacts where you are able to critically discuss new ideas. This can also be an international group where you can send your ideas and questions to each other via email.

"What to Do and What to Let Others Do"

By Anke Meyer-Grashorn

Why are some businesses more successful than others? How do they succeed in navigating the arduous path from ideas to innovation? Why do organizations need personalities like Regina Mehler, who transform mere musings into successful products and services? Unfortunately, there is no patented recipe. However, some of the most important aspects that contribute to innovational success have become apparent to me through cooperation with Adobe Systems and other prosperous, innovative companies.

Innovation in an innovative business is a question of culture. How can you recognize when a business practices an innovative business culture? Simple: When innovation is totally normal for them.

In businesses without an innovative culture, alarm bells often ring when the word innovation is mentioned, signaling an extraordinary condition. Teams are then ripped from their normal work flow, as special task forces are created for a secret mission, in order to devise a plan that will decide the fate of the entire organization, if not the entire world. The people who don't participate in this secret mission, rarely hear about it. The people who did participate are appeased after one or two days and the extraordinary situation is successfully over, leaving them to continue working mundanely, like before the Alarm of Innovation. One time, when I was visiting 3M, creators of Post-Its and other innovations, I rang the reception and asked to speak with a representative for Innovation. The woman on the other end of the line laughed and said, "At 3M, everyone is innovative!" Now that's what I call an innovative business culture!

In the following paragraphs, I will summarize what the key requirements are (from my experience), that help a business generate innovations from ideas. Not all of the points should be enacted in their entirety in some industries, due to the fact that concrete outcomes vary even in everyday business. This is more of a collection of important criteria that are proven to contribute to the innovational success of a company and how you can accomplish the essential framework for them.

■ Innovation is part of a company's philosophy

Innovation should be anchored to words like "value" and "goal" in writing, whether it be in the vision or mission statements of a company or the guiding principles, target agreements, or something similar. Innovation is a company policy decision, part of the company's philosophy and a company culture. An innovative culture in the entire company is the basis of innovation actually occurring and someone having the trust in themselves to bring new ideas into the game. One cannot decree a business culture right away – it is a process that takes time and requires the engagement of all parties involved.

For example, an openly acknowledged recognition of innovation by successful companies is found on their website, and the word innovation is often in the first (or at the very least, second) page of the research and development section.

- **STRATEGY AND SYSTEMS UNDERLIE INNOVATION**

Strategy means determining goals and a clear course of action to obtain innovation, which is also measurable for improvement purposes. Many successful companies set innovative quotas, for example, what percent of the products are allowed to be older than 3 years, or what percentage of the profits must come from new products. System means that the whole thing is not an accident, but rather an efficient process that is explainable, measurable, improvable, and able to be appraised.

- **INNOVATION NEEDS CARETAKERS AND ROLE MODELS**

Innovation is a manager's task and is clearly an executive function. Innovation needs someone that will care for it, feel responsible for it, and take it personally. Being a manager's task doesn't mean that the CEO or other executives have to spew ideas, the entire day, themselves. This means that the executives should, rather, recognize the importance of this theme and the use of collective efforts, and that they inspire their colleagues on a daily basis. Even good innovation processes fail when they lack the personal attention from upper level management.

- **INNOVATION NEEDS TIME, SPACE, AND RESOURCES**

Innovation is no mistake and is not created in passing, when everything serious is already taken care of. Daily routine is the enemy of creative thinking. Innovators need a free space in which is possible to think differently and that provides a perfect balance of relaxation, concentration, security, and stimulation. Innovators also need time in order to develop their ideas and create innovation out of them. In some companies, free time is given in the form of special days. For example, one day in the week where employees can busy themselves with new ideas, inventions, or products as they wish. Or special rooms are dedicated as thinking rooms or idea corners. There are also regular workshops, presentations, and small but constant units of benchmark and exchanges with other companies (such as in-house conventions) where employees can present their new ideas internally.

- **INNOVATION MEANS ACTIVELY HUNTING AND GATHERING**

Ideas are the requirements for innovation and the competitive edge; they are a valuable possession. Innovative companies are hot for ideas and collect as many of them as they can get. The more, the better. Successful businesses have well-functioning idea management in order to compile the ideas of their employees. They tap into all possible sources, they arrange competitions, and they award prizes. Some even publicize the process and involve their customers and the outside world as external followers in their production of ideas.

- **INNOVATION IS LIFE AND MOVEMENT**

Innovation and the unfamiliar are not static, per se, but rather full of movement and energy. Whether a topic lives and is always present has to deal primarily with communication. Innovation in companies needs comprehensive, in-house communication support and also external support in order to remind everyone again that this is an essential topic that bears a high priority.

- **The Structure of Innovation are Networks, Cooperation, and Partnerships**

Innovative businesses make active networks, conquer departmental thinking and exchange heterogeneous teams with a more cross-departmental hierarchy. They are in contact with interesting positions outside the company. These different impulses and inspirations from both within and externally are the breeding ground for new ideas. In the production of ideas, groups are, many times, more creative and productive than an individual.

- **Innovation Requires Blood, Guts, and Passion**

Actions speak louder than words. The majority of points on this list are nothing new. Ultimately, we know how it's supposed to function. But, what separates innovative companies from less innovative ones is that they act upon their knowledge. They walk the walk. They enter a brave new world with the knowledge that it could turn out bad. No risk, no fun. Without courage, nothing happens. We can find many examples in history books that can attest to that. The ones that weathered the storm and trusted themselves are named there – not the ones who listened to the majority, the "yes, but…" people, or the skeptics.

- **Innovation is Personnel**

Most of these requirements for successful innovation have one thing in common… people! Innovational abilities are personal. Companies aren't innovative, their employees are. "Creativity takes place in within a circumference of 50 square meters" says Ernst Papel, a Munich-based psychologist and neurologist. This confirms what I have found out from many workshops and seminars. Creative thinking and the resulting innovation requires physical proximity, a direct exchange, personal contact, and dialogue between people face-to-face. This creates an energy that sets the process in motion.

Innovation is associated with strong emotional changes – anxiety and bravery among them. We can't shake the connection, but we can change our personal approach to them and decide that we are open to innovation. We can develop methods and tricks to get our insecurities under control and knowingly choose to have courage. We can start small and gradually increase our sense of security when the first success is evident. Then, the following steps are made easier.

When I feel anxious, I calculate the worst case scenario and contemplate what would happen if everything went totally downhill. I intensively visualize myself in that situation and try to imagine myself experiencing it until the bitter end. Then, I decide if I can live with the worst consequences or not. For example, what would happen if I went into the next board meeting with a red clown nose on and started describing my latest ideas on the wall in permanent marker instead of using a flip chart? Maybe I would be laughed at, maybe someone would recommend a good psychiatrist, or maybe they would get angry and throw me out. Maybe I would even lose my most important customers. One thing is certain – I definitely have to repaint the walls at my own cost.

What can I live with, what not? To be laughed at is no problem for me. Until you've lost your reputation, it may sound unabashed. The wall? Comical. The aggravated clients and the damage from the fallout? That hurts. But, when I think a little deeper, someone actually pays me to be different from the rest, and if they get upset because of a clown nose or my musings on the wall, then maybe I should think twice about whether this is a good basis for a long-term business relationship. Maybe it is better to make room for other clients who want to break free from routine and forge a new path. This would be my personal thoughts on this case – I would take the risk.

If you are getting an ulcer from reading this, if you think you can't afford to lose any clients, or if you cringe to consider that someone might laugh at you, save yourself the investment in the clown nose. But, you should consider the following worst-case scenario. What happens when nothing happens and everything stays the same? The consequences that could arise from this worst case are much more serious and are a real risk. Innovating on safe ground is not possible. So just trust your gut and remember that being crazy is a requirement!

Idea-deliverers and Inspiration-givers
How a Good Network Inspires You Professionally and Privately

Whether its motivation, an idea, or an opinion – if I can't get there on my own, I can count on my personal network. This took more than ten years to assemble and it includes all of the people I regularly exchange questions with about jobs and careers. With this group of people, I can really be sure that they give time and thought to anything I ask them concretely. It doesn't just give me a good feeling, it has really helped me to find an appropriate solution to many problems. I can discuss crazy ideas and non-developed thoughts with my network – things that I wouldn't present to a company yet. They can be my test group and, above everything, I can start from their advice and learn with them. The network offers knowledge coupled with competence that I can't compete with as an individual, but that I can use in the network to achieve my goals.

What is different from a team of colleagues and a network is that in a network, there is no common goal and no hierarchy. There's no measurement or comparisons, no competition. Instead, the network is based on a voluntary give and take, paired with fair exchanges that can give every side an advantage. The unwritten contract that exists between networkers is that anyone can ask for support, answers, or opinions at any time, and you will receive it as long as you engage yourself in the network in the same way.

The fascinating thing about this exchange is that in contrast with a team in a company, everyone follows their individual aspirations and, thanks to the network, these are faster and easier to achieve than if you would act on your own. In short, a network is win-win. Everyone profits.

Whether you are looking for an event location in Moscow, a point of contact for questions on the IT infrastructure in Pakistan, or if you need to be put in touch with an astronaut – in a well-functioning marketing network, someone can help you with every request. Or, at least, give some neutral feedback, for example, on a lecture or a PowerPoint presentation that you want to impress your boss with.

In a network, you are able to discuss the management of your employees and your career planning openly – something which you are not able to do in a company. Additionally. a network helps expand the general knowledge of its members. One can be informed quickly and easily about topics that may lie outside of your area of expertise and, therefore, they are inspiring.

> "It's not about what you know, but who you know." –
> UNKNOWN

> "Do something every once in a while where you earn less or maybe even nothing at all – it pays!"
> OLIVER HASSENCAMP

> "Managers in the future will no longer have the role of the do-er – they must be rather the contact point in a network that withstands the test of creative intelligence." –
> Prof. PETER KRUSE

The Network Family

In a society that is becoming more and more anonymous, I think it is more than necessary to build a personal network or to engage yourself in one that already exists. In this fast-paced world, a network is very useful, also as a social function. We change our jobs – voluntarily or involuntarily – and with that we change our social environment as well. Here, a network provides a much-needed constant. We no longer have the stability that our parents had with their employers – that has gradually decreased over the years to a point of non-existence. However, we still need a social basis and the security that comes with it, just like in the past.

Networks are a good platform to expand upon your own knowledge and become a high performer (and stay one.) Your career requires constant learning and, in many areas, new ideas are also always required. If you want to stick it out, you have to know the best practices. Which ones are the most current in a company, I can only discover when I think outside of the box.

Idea-deliverers and Inspiration-givers

A network can also help to make your own career more exciting. Whoever works with recurring projects and processes and feels unchallenged as a result can find important inspiration in a network. When you approach new projects, you become more motivated, and, as a result, your work life takes a more interesting shape. Many networks noticed a book during the crisis of 2008 and 2009. Xing, a German social network for professionals, saw an increase of 45% in their memberships (raising their total members to 7 million) and an 80% increase in their profits (totaling 35 million Euro). By 2009, there were 8.75 million members (a 26% increase from the year before) and the company recorded a 45 million Euro profit.

"My friends are my fortune." –
EMILY DICKINSON

Unavoidable and Indispensable – the Personal Contact Environment

If you currently belong to the group of people who are not purposefully building and caring for their network, then you can still relax, because, although it might be unbeknownst to you, you already have a network. You can hardly avoid networking. Everyone has had ties to contacts during their education and training that they used to exchange information about various topics. In school, you have exchanged notes and questions about tests. At the job application stage, you traded interview and resume tips – without ever developing a more personal friendship. However later, the contact might be reestablished, perhaps by one person referring the other to a company or exchanging information about an employer or new advanced training possibilities. You can and should expand systematically on this already existing network.

Next, a couple of thoughts on the definition of a network. A network is a congregation of people with the goal of learning in a group. It is, to some extent, a stock market for the exchange of ideas and information. Members want to discuss and learn from the experience of others. A network relies on

"Keep away from people who try to belittle your ambitions. Small people alwys do that, but the really great make you feel that you, too, can become great." –
MARK TWAIN

the growth of ideas, knowledge, and contacts. There, one can interact with others freely. A network is not limited to a particular circle, but is always expanding in order to improve its level of efficiency. That's how a high level of competence is guaranteed. Whoever is open to new contacts and ideas can continuously expand their horizons.

Sustainability Pays

Networks want to be invested in for the long term. Obtaining new clients and winning commissions are not things that you will receive in a one-way mode. It's the opposite – the most unwritten network rules forbid this. So, it is taboo to join a network where you can acquire knowledge but you can't bring anything to the group yourself. Unfortunately, this happens often and it degrades the value of the network to the point where they become auctions for the highest bidder. In a network where you want to profit long term, it's different. There, you can:

- Learn from people whose conduct and results have incited your curiosity
- Exchange information and find out, in particular, where your strengths and weaknesses are in comparison to others
- Develop new ideas through exchanges with others
- Bring your own opinions and your own knowledge to the group

"Whoever uses networking as a platform to sell his huge product line, will fail." –
BRIGITTE ETTL, Business Coach

The openness and willingness to constantly expand your knowledge separates a network from followers. The followers come in and then opt out, due to the fact that the quality of the network has been damaged and new contacts are seldom joining. The network functions better, the more people that join from different job fields, since they can integrate with different backgrounds. The more diverse the contacts, the more inspiration. Part of your network can be your work colleagues, whether you want that or not, you must decide for yourself. You must simply consider that one or two questions may arise about your career – and maybe you do not wish to speak about them amongst your colleagues.

Therefore, I am active in not just one, but many networks. At the European Marketing Expert Network, I am continuously finding inspiration. I am also interested in management networks. Additionally, I am a member of networks where I meet many members from different industries: alternative medicine practitioners, investment bankers, architects or CEOs. There are many specialized networks for those who work in specialized trades or for young entrepreneurs. Also, the women's business club, which offers many nice possibilities to acquire contacts from all different industries and branches. By the way, I pull my most creative ideas from this group.

> "The internet is not for sale – it was created rather for the communication between humanity."
> FERI THIERRY, Political Advisor

Real, Virtual, or Mixed

In the current times of web 2.0 and social media, personal meetings (face-to-face) are not always required to maintain contact. Whether on Twitter, Facebook, Linkedin or Xing, you are able to stay linked to old colleagues or current business partners and use these platforms as a discussion forum for different themes.

Right Click – Your First Links for New Network Options

I find the mix of personal contact and digital communication particularly effective. There are people in my network that I have only met once or twice personally, but I regularly exchange information with them via email. This is useful and good. What is really exciting is when I get to experience the contact in my network as people, not just as information-givers and inspiration-bringers. In the corporate world, we are

> "It doesn't hurt when strengths are strengthened." –
> JOHANN WOLFGANG VON GOETHE

used to looking at function and efficiency, but your professional life is only fun if it affords you positive encounters with others. The collective solution to a task, a mutual success, a shared experience. You know the saying, "Business was created by people"? So were networks.

The more personally I know my network and the longer I have them, the more valuable they are. From this, I have created my inner circle, which is so stable and close to me, that I can even ask the most sensitive questions about business or any other topics. The inner circle functions like a friendship, created and based upon long standing trust that enables an immeasurable and deep exchange.

> "Trustful relationships are built where you give them room." – Tom Noeding

Give and Take as a Principle

Good networks are based on a fair exchange. In every network, everyone must give input. If you join a network and only focus on obtaining as much information for yourself as possible, you won't be successful. Instead, you must be prepared to bring your own knowledge and know-how into the group. The first step is to begin to speak about your own motivation, your own successes, and your current job description. And then, suddenly, you don't just want to get to know your contacts in the network, but rather the members as people.

This is often more difficult than it sounds, especially in face-to-face talks. This requires practice from your side to recount career development, hard questions you have faced, and the solutions you found. Cross my heart, that it won't hurt you. Under most circumstances, it just takes a little time to let yourself get used to it. No one should be insecure about this, because it is like that with everyone, even me. Even today, after ten years of successful networking, I still have to give myself a little push when I visit an event where I have to meet new people. This is probably based on the innate shyness that every human experiences. For Neanderthals and other an-

> "Whoever wants to start a network must look for people who have fun with change, are hungry for something new, and who are ready to enter new territory. Skeptics cannot create a network." – HANS-CHRISTIAN BLUNK, Business Advisor

cients, wariness towards foreign people was a survival tactic. I fight this internal feeling with a touch of rationality. I consciously acknowledge that all of the other attendees will find themselves in the same situation as me – they are looking for new contacts, they rarely know anyone here, and even if they appear to be chatting away in happy little groups, they probably have all just met each other.

In networks that regularly organize personal meetings, the possibilities of getting yourself in are remarkably large. For example, in some networks, they request members to give a presentation. If you are asked, take the chance and say "yes". Maybe the network is looking for a space for an evening event. If possible, volunteer some space at your office. Or, maybe someone is looking for a good caterer or a wine supplier – if you see a good opportunity to support, do it. The more you involve yourself, the more well-known you will be and the easier it will be to secure other contacts. Then, you will really start to enjoy yourself and you will find the network to be more useful to you.

There have been times where I, as a marketer, was looking for agencies or press contacts in different countries. I would casually ask my network and suddenly I'd have a list of valuable proposals. In business, it is also sometimes like your private life, where you ask your friends for a restaurant or gym recommendation – you can use others like the Yellow Pages.

> "Networking means sending out into the system what we know, and having it return to recirculate continually through the network." – WAYNE DYER

Network Outside of the Box

I already told you, networks that are colorfully mixed, not just organized by industries or branches, can be more valuable than others – whether it is a golf club, rotary, or a women's network. Accountants can meet artists, policemen can meet pediatricians, teachers can meet telemarketers. And that's what makes it exciting – because encounters with people from different fields often give you the best inspiration.

> "It is the encounters with others that makes life worth living." – GUY DE MAUPASSANT

I am lucky to count artist, Theresa Hebenstreit, among my network members. In her piece, *1001 Naked*, she created 1001 figurines that personify women. Every one was a completely different size and shape, but still, each other had one fascinating similarity. Theresa displayed these 1001 figures throughout the world, most notably in China, and financed the exhibitions through sponsors. Each buyer held an option on the figurine, that increased in value as the exhibitions went on. Suddenly, Therese has sold almost all of the figurines in advance. This idea fascinates me, and I wonder if there is something to learn here: Now and then a story about advance financing a project would be useful for us marketers.

Kick-off Your Personal Networking Project

> "Even if the structure is attractive, networking is work and costs time." –
> BRIGITTE ETTL

When you are motivated to expand your network, approach this with your contacts that already exist. The best would be to organize your own personal networking project like you would organize a project at work. You plan it, set measures in place, and then monitor your success. Whoever acts sporadically, focused on the short term, will never expand their network.

A good starting point would be, for example, your comrades from your student days that have scattered in the wind, landing at different companies. It is worth it to look them up. Alumni networks from universities can also help, many old colleagues are up for grabs. Maybe there are other organizations that existed during your time at school that still exist now and could present an opportunity to rebuild contacts, like the international student organization, AIESEC. If you have never found the time to attend an alumni event before, participate in the next one. It also makes sense to ask your work colleagues if they participate in one – maybe they want to connect. In some networks, you have to be referred. One organization in Munich requires three referrals in order to be granted admission. Therefore, it might be better to begin the second step of the network project.

Find the Right Network

Networks are experiencing a boom. The challenge is finding out which one is right for you. Therefore, you have to define your goals, just like with any project.

- What exactly do you want to achieve through networking? Is it about asking general questions (about career development, looking for a mentor or starting in a new city) or are you looking for answers to specific questions?
- Are you looking for an international network? There are a variety of business clubs that are active in Europe and worldwide so that you have access to their network in other countries, for example, when you travel on business.
- What type of network is right for you? What fits in best with your everyday life? Business card exchanges, field events, networking breakfasts, golf trips, and lunch meetings are all possibilities.
- Where do you feel best – in large or small groups?
- How much time do you have to invest?

If you have figured out the answers to the above questions, you can begin your network search. When you enter key words like Business Club, Networking and your city or region, you will most likely find an abundance of results. You should compare the characteristics of your search results with the requirements you have laid out for yourself from the above questions. Also, consider the many social networks that you probably already belong to but are inactive in the discussions. Maybe become a participant in blogs or join Twitter, Xing, LinkedIn and Facebook if you haven't already. Take the knowledge that you can offer and bring it into these networks.

Keep Calm and Remain Patient

Once you have selected your desired sphere of influence, you can move onto the next step and test the network. I recommend visiting every network at least three or four times, to get a solid impression of the content, members, and structure. Even if your first impression is that the network doesn't offer what you expected, you should continue to go. Because the on first networking evening, you will rarely meet that business partner you have been looking for, even the next lunch is not enough time to stimulate the proper talks and the first of many golf tournaments don't always lead to additional income. In my opinion, there is only one reason to prematurely eliminate a network: the environment and the members do not convenience you. It's very important that you feel confident and good about your first conquest. That is the minimum requirement for your networking success.

Points of contact at events often present themselves. As a rule, a presentation is normally given that requires discussion among the audience. Most often, the presenter is then surrounded by participants after the presentation. Go right up to this group and you will automatically become involved in conversation with the others.

It is more difficult to pick the right contacts from the many people that you will meet. This is where your intuition comes into play: your gut knows in the first two to four seconds if the person across from you is pleasant or not, or if they are exciting or boring. Go with your gut – this is not much different from how you would handle things in your private life.

A Regimen for the Advanced

When you feel more secure, you can begin a regime. The regime is going from table to table during a networking event and giving yourself a brief summary of the network members. While doing so, bring yourself into the conversation and if an opportunity presents itself, introduce yourself. When you want to end the conversation, you don't need to have any scruples, as long as you don't turn the event into speed dating. Give the person you are talking to some time and room, but when you feel that you have made an impression, and everything has been said for this day, you may kindly and politely make your departure, stating that you would like to speak with one or two other people. And that is how you participate. The bar tables – a must for any networking event so that the participants can get to know each other – give you the mobility that you need. When you are standing, you are able to change more spontaneously to another table than if you were sitting in a lounge chair. Even the most successful business personalities know this: at a networking event, the goal is not to acquire a high amount of new contacts. The best conversations come unexpectedly. A certain placidity affords you more than being fixed on a specific goal.

Networking is linked with regular expenses. Emphasis on the word "regular." For participants in networking events, I recommend investing one or two evenings a week in the beginning. I am currently partaking in three to four networking events per month, that I arrange myself through on to one meetings. If you are active in a similar fashion, you will have built your personal network (that supports you professionally and privately) in about two years. You will know who you can turn to when you have questions and whether they are about a financial concept, a marketing idea, or a diving school.

Last But Not Least: the Costs

For years, I paid the membership fees of my networks myself, because I thought that networking was my personal indulgent. Now, I see it differently: my employer profits just as much as I do through my contacts. As the head of marketing,

> "At the end, it's about meeting people. Personal contacts are priceless" –
> HASSO PLATTNER, SAP AG

I bring new ideas, exciting speakers and the best vendors to my work, thanks to the network.

In my company, we discuss marketing options that I pulled from the network as ideas. We expanded on an idea that I took from a networking colleague and ended up developing "Marketing Lectures" – an informational forum for clients and employees. I wanted to bring new trends into the company as a series, to inform my colleagues and motivate them to new ideas. I discussed this proposition with a PR expert from my network, who encouraged me to organize these lectures and market them regularly. Now, we are on the third year of the series and they have become so popular that not just employees, but customers, partners, agencies, journalists, and analysts participate. This amazed my employer, and now they cover a part of my networking costs. I have already set aside part of my budget to fund the networking costs of my own employees.

Parallel to the networking boom, I have noticed an overall increase in appreciation for networking from the side of the company. More often than not, the executives know that it is absolutely vital, especially for sales employees, to anchor themselves in the customer's environment. Whether it's a convention, a sales congress or an in-house event, they are an obligations for those in sales. And how it concerns marketing can be seen when a marketer stays in contact with colleagues from other companies.

> "The quality of the personal relationships in enterprises and corporations will ultimately be the deciding factor in competitive advantage." –
> LEO A. NEFODIOW, Analyst

Ten Tips for Successful Marketing

Be aware that you have to invest time regularly. The positive about this is that is how you practice, and when you regularly visit a networking event, the other members will eventually start approaching you themselves.

- Be open and tolerant.
- Train yourself to approach strangers. Think that they too much conquer their fear of the unknown to approach you as well.
- Maintain contacts from completely different branches and industries. You often get the best ideas from these connections.
- Ask your colleagues and business contacts if they would accompany you to an established event. They will definitely ask you to return the favor, one day.
- Set goals for yourself. In the beginning, I recommend testing two to three networks. Where do you feel good? Where don't you?
- Listen actively. Ask follow-up questions and think about whether you can help the person that you are speaking with.
- Be patient. You often don't know the real value of a contact right away.
- If you get something, give something back in return. A network is based on win-win.
- Engage yourself actively in networking – give presentations, bring in new topics, or initiate a sporting event. Then, you will be more well-known and easily integrated into the network.
- Four Absolute Networking Don'ts
- Don't solicit or present any products during your first contact. This degrades the networking event down to a sales convention.
- Don't succumb to attending events that don't give you enjoyment – it's a waste of time.
- Don't hold on to contacts that don't work for you, even if the position of the contact or their topic of expertise is important for you. If you feel weird about something, it could get stressful, and it shouldn't be like that.
- Don't hold short, concise discussions with others and then move on to the next. This isn't speed dating and at a networking event it is unsophisticated and rude.

> "Networking means sending out into the system what we have and what we know, and having it return to recirculate continually through the network." –
> WAYNE DYER

"Important People Have Important Contacts"

By Monika Scheddin

By now, everyone should have realized that your success in business is reliant upon networking.

Employees can score original ideas when they network in different branches. Also, they can experience an amazing amount of competitive edge if they bring new contacts into a company when they are changing jobs. But membership in a junior business club, a marketing club, or even a thousand Xing contacts will not make a different if they are not constituted with good intent.

In terms of networking, workers are pretty timid – only a maximum 20% of you network outside of your company and outside of your industry. It's obvious that 80% of all contractors and self-employed people are avid networkers; they are dependent upon finding new customers, new suppliers, and require exciting new ideas, preferably before their competition. They profit naturally from exchanges and benchmarking.

So how do you find the right contacts or network partners that will bring you further? In this position, I can offer you four Scheddinisms (my formulas):

- Always network on the same level or higher. Find out where the people that are where you want to be hang out. Get in contact with these people and find out what their success concepts are. Learn from them and try to avoid their mistakes, even if this sounds outlandish to you. When building your carrier, you want to achieve goals, not conduct social work. You should keep your social life private. Therefore, don't network below yourself or with people who are where you once were, unless they are part of your target group or you are participating in an official mentoring group, but there, you need to follow the first rule of thumb and cultivate your mentoring colleagues, instead of enhancing your network.

- In order to ripen a relationship, you need an average of two years and seven contacts. Many people think that it is acceptable to present a product or service to an important decision maker after only meeting him or her once. "I hate that – it's like a prey being hunted. I immediately lose interest in my conversation partner", one decision maker from a DAX 30 company told me. Therefore, you need to develop real interest, calculate your timing and behave more humanely.
- Acquire one new contact per week and continue cultivating one existing contact. You are probably thinking to yourself, "52 contacts a year?" and that feels like a lot of work. But guess what? Networking is work. You will really need a critical amount of contacts so that you can fish out the really interesting ones. From approximately 52 contacts a year, on average, only 10% will be worth keeping – if you are lucky. That's about 5 people per year and these will be really quality contacts.
- Important people have important contacts. This is a rule of thumb that may save you a lot of work. Profiteers, who only serve themselves, will become apparent when they receive something for free and after many years, still haven't returned the favor. Surround yourself with people that you can rely on instead; people that are there for you. Then, you will have people on the same wavelength as yourself.

In order to be so good at something that you are considered an expert, you need to invest 10,000 hours in that subject. In other words, power / authority amounts to about 10 years. That goes for businesses as well as networkers. With the exception of being a networking expert, for which you need to network about 20 hours a week. Sound over-exaggerated?

Week A:	
2 hours	Weekly golf training with clients
6 hours	Presentation, including breakfast with VIP guests the next day
10 hours	Your own advanced training
2 hours	Lecture on Networking
Week B:	
3 days	3 day excursion with clients
Week C:	
4 hours	Business Club meeting
4 hours	Client Event
2 hours	Various telephone conversations
3 hours	Send out a newsletter and follow up
2 hours	Write a blog entry
2 hours	Tweet networking news
3 hours	Dinner with clients

Network Progression

2 Years of Networking	Build your foundation Identify your platforms, become a member in an industry-related network, and also become a member in a cross-industry, cross-departmental network
5 Years of Networking	Make your Mark You have earned a positive reputation in your network and have built your own personal network

10 Years of Networking	Quality Networking You have moved into the premium area and have been invited into the exclusive, private circles. You can combine networking activities with your on personal interests (for example, a mountain tour or a golf event).
30 Years of Networking	Harvest Time You are now Mr. or Mrs. Networking. New acquisitions are no longer necessary. You have a considerable amount of leverage; you sit on the advisory board and are finally earning money from networking.

In the last couple of years, Herbert Seckler, founder of the famous Sansibar restaurant, and Thomas Sabo, a jewelry designer, have become more and more well-known. Suddenly, they are present in the business and celebrity scene. Suddenly? No way. Both have been in business for over 30 years, and it takes that long to break into the market and make a name for yourself.

Herbert Seckler began his gastronomic empire with a small stand on the beach in Sylt and by now he has accommodated almost every prominent person with status. But he really makes his money with lifestyle textiles and what you can hardly believe… a line of pet clothing that is sold under his label. Does he produce this himself? Of course not. Herbert Seckler contracts licenses for products that he likes. He also earns money with networking, and rightly so. His whole operation, his ideas, and his perseverance have made him rich. As a successful business man, he has raised his power of attraction so high that others want to sell their products under his successful Sansibar brand.

When I met Herbert Seckler personally in 2009 at a

media network round table, two things immediately made an impression on me:

He's an oddball. He doesn't like to travel so he doesn't do it. Even for a high quality televised interview with certain public relations consequences.

He is generous and you can take his word. If he agrees to something, then he holds himself to it. And when he makes an appearance, there is always a lot of time and attention given, along with many rounds of champagne.

Generosity and the value of brand recognition (as well as being odd) are typical characteristics of a good networker. Being generous means giving back to others (buying a product from them, use their services or recommend them for something), as soon as you are in the position to do so. It also means being a good host – in person or virtually. Being odd makes you interesting and unpredictable. Herbert Seckler never runs the risk of being too engaged or overexposed in the mainstream.

The Win-Win Myth

When I recommend someone, they should orientate themselves upwards in their network cultivation and ask themselves the question, "What do the people that I want to meet get in return from meeting with me?" At first, nothing. Therefore, it's up to you to make the meeting palatable. For example, honest praise and compliments, indication of a positive review on Amazon of their recent book, an invitation to an original restaurant in a location favorable to your desired contact. Or invite your contact as a guest to a carefully selected group of people meeting for drinks. This suggestion is favorable to most people, we've noticed from the quality networking platform "Good People's Lunch".

No one does anything without a reason. A service in return is always desired. If only in the form of a positive observation.

Too often is the reference to win-win just an excuse for not giving a service in return. You need to actually thank people with a nice gift, a bouquet of flowers, an original invitation, or with a commission if they have recommended customers to you. This is also networking. These recommendations have certainly done you a favor and there are aspects of both obligation and enjoyment involved.

The wonderful planning manager Pero Micis wrote in the prologue for my networking book, "Above all, networking means creating a future with pleasant and interesting people." This is a really excellent definition of networking for me. Products and services are interchangeable, but people are not.

Networking is unintentional intent. Networkers are not people with boredom. Of course, they are pursuing their goals. But they become successful when they forget this goal for a moment and they involve themselves in their target group. They win by doing this because they have respect and esteem for other people, and their topics then interest others.

Cooperation with Other Companies
The Advantage of Business Partnerships

You've probably recognized this by now: I am a convicted advocate of professional exchanges and cooperation between people. Therefore, as a consequence, I am also a supporter of cooperation between businesses, in any shape and form. Since, what makes more sense than to work together towards your common goals? For example, the hardware from your company works optimally with a software solution from another company, and without this, you wouldn't be able to reach your target group. Or, an automobile manufacturer and another provider team up to produce the perfect car. Or the Star Alliance concept from Lufthansa. They are not able to service the same route under the Star Alliance all alone, so they searched for business partners to expand their portfolio. Also, for example, to bundle flights with hotels and rentals cars to offer weekend escapes.

The IT industry relies on partnerships to a huge extent. Almost every IT company cooperates in one form or another. Together, they execute marketing campaigns, invite customers to events, or alternate their Silver, Gold, or Platinum sponsorships of conventions and partner events.

> "Coming together is a beginning; keeping together is progress; working together is success." – Henry Ford

They all know that a goal can be achieved faster together, rather than alone, and for every requirement there is an appropriate form of partnership.

A goal of an alliance can be, for example, tapping into a new market together. The advantage is that it works faster together and each participant's expense is lower. If two companies can synchronize their products together, then the packet for the customer is especially lucrative. Also, a common execution of an event can lead to double the amount of visitors.

Just like networking, cooperation between businesses is

based on a give and take relationship. A serious and successful software company needs a business partner that works solidly and is competent in its field. And also the other way around: a business partner with a good client base would never sell software that promises more than it can deliver.

The cooperation serves to enhance the service abilities of each partner. So each side has to precisely state which service they are willing and able to bring into the partnership, and then deliver this reliably. The adherence to the agreement can be a matter of honor or could be regulated by a contract. However, there is no obligation to always have a contract.

Cooperation and partnerships can be built upon different projects and content. Projects with a partner, as well as a common marketing offer, are possibilities. The latter can lead to an independent part of daily business or could be an outstanding project.

A good example of the effect of cooperation between four very strong partners is the IT Vision Tour 2020, which I will explain in detail below. Not one of the partners involved could have pulled on this project – which included a visit from Bill Gates himself.

Appointment with Bill Gates: a Chronology of a Partner Revolution

Inter-business cooperation can be the platform to achieve extraordinary projects, as many proposals require not just a large budget but big names, that is to say, a demonstration of conglomerate reputations. For example, if you want to invite 25 CIOs from the top European companies to a one week long IT Vision Tour in the USA, and get Bill Gates to the round table, most often, you can't do something like this alone. For this, you need partners, and in this case, it was four: my previous employer (a software manufacturer for customer relationship management) and three other leading software companies with whom we already had developed a service level cooperation. The common executive contacts, we don't use just yet.

It was clear to everyone who participated in the project development that only if the desired attendees were offered something unique, something that would pull in additional value for their area of responsibility, would they grace us with their presence and attention.

So what type of added value does an IT company or a CIO look for? It's obvious: they want to know everything about the trends of the future and new technologies.

An IT leader has on average a seven or eight figure yearly budget at his disposal. For him, it is essential to find out how to invest this money wisely to get the highest possible return.

This was the basic thought behind our mega-project. From there, we were going to develop the idea to create a C-level platform where people would be able to discuss the future of the IT industry. This platform should be so embarrassingly attractive that all of the CIOs wanted to participate without a doubt. Logically, we came to the conclusion that which location could be more inspiring than the epicenter of all IT innovation itself? Silicon Valley in California. Now we had the "where". In the process, we also decided how long the event should last: the appropriate time frame would have to be about a week. Therefore, we were going to invite people to a one week long IT Vision 2020 Tour.

We quickly agreed on the "who" question as well – executives from the top 25 European IT companies were on our list. The *only* thing still in question was the highlight that would attract these people. A top-level IT person would only participate in this event if he is offered the chance of productive networking and if there was a particularly enticing attraction. We wanted to offer both.

The participants of this tour were supposed to visit the businesses who created the event (our company and our three other partners) for one day and speak with the various c-levels there to exchange ideas about their visions of the business in the next 15 years. This alone was an interesting option for the IT executives, since you can't say "no" to a trip with that many high-quality contacts involved. The concept promised real value for our contacts and was only made possible due to the fact that we bundled power with strategic partnerships. While all of the four partner businesses were tapping into their contacts together, we brought not just the IT executives from the top 25 IT companies, but also the US executives from the leading worldwide software houses. The result? Bill Gates wanted to speak with us – and not just because Microsoft was a partner of this party, but we placed a concentrated top-level event on his radar.

The Microsoft founder invited the top 25 participating CIOs, representing businesses in the telecommunications, automotive, financial, and trade industries, to meet with him. And, as expected, the meeting with Bill Gates was the highlight of the trip. Gates, a reserved man whose charisma was in full effect on the stage, presented his vision of his company in the next decade. He took more than three hours' time, excited about the deepness of the discussion. He also let each participant take a personal photo with him and gave them an autograph.

In the end, we marketers and partners of this event had a real cause for rejoicing. The "C-Level Platform" project was a success. Thanks to the presentations and discussions, the participants received insight into the visions of the companies and more security for their investment decisions. Even today, contacts that were made during this trip still exist across many borders. A concept that this tour was based on was that this offered opportunities to secure deeper relationships.

A major part of the preparation for this event wasn't just the organization of the trip, but the negotiations of the contracts. In them, every detail was laid out – the sponsorship from each partner, the executive speaker representative from the partner, and their exact engagement and commitment.

In addition, each partner was asked to acquire a specific

amount of executive contacts from their customers. They then had a designative key that gave them specific priority to follow-up with these leads. During the first transition, this all seemed so painstaking and detail-oriented. But, when you consider that each contact could potentially bring in 6 digit revenue figures, then it makes sense to deliberate the conditions and how you would handle everything in advance.

A Cooperation Model

It doesn't have to be about a Bill Gates Tour; cooperation is always meaningful when it comes to day-to-day business or small projects. Here is a selection of possible models:

A Solution Partnership

This is a partnership where one company brings in a product and the second company is able to customize that product (offer a solution) for a customer's particular circumstances, where the corresponding solution is integrated. Famous example: SAP. The SAP solutions are implemented by companies on location, not just by SAP employees. Instead, there are many small and large consulting houses, which tend to the implementation. Often times these projects are middle to long-term tasks, which means that the cooperation between the two companies can also be long-term.

For marketing, that means that you are able to bundle offers from both sides. A bigger budget comes together and the market is targeted more efficiently.

For example, a software manufacturer and the implementation partner invite target customers to an event. The software manufacturer reports on the product and the partner recounts a recently completed project. For the visitor, this event is especially interesting because they are able to see the product in action. The manufacturer informs the target group at length about the product, and the partner extensively details the practice example. All-in-all, it's a compact informational event that generates interest.

Not just that, but the cooperation is attractive for the manufacturer and the partner company, because they can host the event together. The costs are then cut in half and this leads to a bigger data flow and more profit in the end.

Channel Partnership / Sales Partnership

A channel partnership's goal is to position a big amount of product on the market. For such partnerships, most manufacturers offer a multi-component program, including certifications, partner classifications, and a bonus system. With this form of cooperation, there are the classic work divisions. The manufacturer takes care of the market expansion, while the channel partner looks after the local market for which he normally receives marketing development funds.

Strategic Partnerships

This is a long-term oriented cooperation where both partners can develop solutions together. A partnership like this is most often entered into when a big project is at stake. Quite often, the client can name the partners. Marketing also comes into play in this cooperation, to support with "Named Account Marketing" (which means a specific marketing plan is developed for this important customer). A strategic plan for this special account is developed in conjunction with the sales department. This can be an e-mail campaign for this account's already existing contacts that invites them to an e-Seminar and then, possibly, a live event. In this case, everything (the email, the seminar, and the live event) are tailored specfically for the client. The advantage is obvious – the most current topics on the client's agenda can be addressed.

Worldwide strategic partnerships are also common between companies and can be transmitted into the local markets. As soon as marketing and sales have defined the first target markets and accounts, it is marketing's tasks to develop and follow-up with the go-to-market plan.

Here, methodical planning is necessary, especially if you want to break into a specific targeted market. Like every big project, you begin to analyze where you stand, who has already achieved penetration of the market, and how the milestones look. From this base, you can develop a strategic marketing plan that can, of course, lead to a longer commitment.

Tactical Partnerships

The partnerships are designed to stimulate revenue in a short amount of time by employing a campaign. Therefore, a company is only looking for other partners who have interest in working together on this deal for the moment.

In this case, it's all about developing short-term marketing campaigns for the partner that can be implemented without much effort on their side. From the ready-made email campaigns on the easy to use campaign website to Christmas deals with the store displays, almost anything is possible. The goal is to impress the partners with the marketing campaign and present the most feasible plan that can generate the most successful results. These offers are sometimes required to correct the figures and bring in extra revenue that is lacking at the end of the quarter.

On the Hunt for a Partner…

What developed as a "must" on the internet when searching for a dating partner is also a requirement in the business world – the creation of a profile. Without precise specifications, it won't work. For whoever is seeking a partnership of another company, must be able to define and articulate their requirements.

In order to make the decision about entering into a partnership, you should choose the same way you would select a new employee. You want to deliberate carefully and it shouldn't be a decision from your department alone, but rather a collective decision involving the entire business. In order for the partnership to function, all departments should work together, or it will lead to conflict.

I can remember a trade fair appearance with an implementation partner that I did in a previous position. Everything was clear on the side of the marketing department; We had developed a common concept for propositioning customers and we had a clear plan to bring customers to the booth. Everything worked wonderfully. When the convention began, a crowd of people rushed to the booth and there were so many people that the sales team couldn't keep up with those who had interest. But, instead of celebrating the big success on the first evening, there was a fight amongst the sales team for the leads (the contact information from the target partners). The cause: the members of our partner's sales team suspected one of our colleagues of stealing contact information for his own benefit, because he didn't register the information at the centralized collection point (a really outrageous suspicion). This sales colleague was one of our best and this was so far from the truth. He was a really engaged man who was the contact personally requested by many of the people visiting the stand – much more than the others. Since the day was so hectic, he had forgotten to forward the information to the central collection point.

Looking back, I think the real problem was that the sales teams didn't really know one another. If they had agreed to meet and discuss everything before the trade fair, perhaps this wouldn't have happened. If the base of trust would have already existed, this organizational problem could have been avoided.

With much effort, we were able to convince the partner, in

the end, that a lack of time had caused this misunderstanding. All's well that ends well and a few years later the partner ended up recruiting the very salesman that they so unattractively accused.

This example shows that a solid partnership is not the result of a single marketing or sales initiative, but rather a collective effort between all departments. Exactly which management level should have the final sign-off is dependent upon which qualities and which time scale the partnership is measured by. The rule of thumb is that the more strategy and time that is invested in the partnership, the higher the level of the deciding department. But, even when the decision is finally brought to top management, both sides must meet with all of the employees that this decision will affect. Therefore, it is important to engage marketing and sales departments from both companies in the decision process as early as possible, for it is those employees that put forth the most effort and will be the most important players in the day-to-day business of this cooperation. Depending on the size of the first project, this should be in the elaborate contract. Alternatively, one can initially do several independent pilots, in order to contractually fix the cooperation at a later point.

Eight Tips for Your Partner Search
- Precisely define what you expect from your partner. Do you want more revenue? Do you want to expand your sales network? Do you want to break into new markets? Do you want to acquire new contacts of customers?
- Define when this partnership is able to be valuable to your success. Does the revenue have to increase? Do you need to see growth in new markets? Do the marketing budgets have to increase due to new common marketing requirements?
- Look for new opportunities with your current partners. Is there something in your sales partner's company that you can present to a new market?

- In case no new opportunities exists with your old partners, which new partnerships can you build?
- Make sure that any new partners fit into your portfolio. Would there eventually be any competition between your potential partner and your current one?
- Create a business plan with your new partner. Define, together, how much growth or advantage is possible and realistic from both sides. But also define the expense that is possible for both sides.
- Speak with the other partners that your potential partner does business with to see how engaged they are in everyday business.
- Celebrate mutual successes with each other. This strengthens the partnership and this is a nice opportunity to think about the next project.

Clear Words, Clear Rules

In order to create a common ground, the goals for each participant in a partnership must be crystal clear. It was really helpful for us during the IT-Vision-2020-Tour to have all of the dates, mission statements, necessary investments, project plans, and a timeline, along with each party's monetary engagement, strictly outlined in the contract. In addition, we also fixed the way that we would handle the resulting contacts from the tour and how to divide the profitability fairly among the partners in advance. As you may remember, dividing up profits or leads can sometimes lead to a conflict.

Often times, there is a false belief that the event (in this case, the one week tour) is the actual goal of the project, but that is too short-sighted. The completion of the project itself is simply the first measure of success. The full success is only achieved when the collected contact information generates serious interest in the business and then finally leads to revenue on the books.

Someone Has to Wear the Hat

The biggest danger to the success of cooperation is that at first there is tons of enthusiasm for the topics and projects, but then this dissipates little by little. Therefore, each cooperation / project / organization, regardless of its form, needs an engaged project leader who focuses on goals, pushes things through, and enforces adherence to the timelines. If not, the project runs the risk of failure.

The most important task of a project leader is generating motivation. If engagement is lacking from one side of the partnership, he needs to bring everyone back to the table and refocus them on the original idea. For this, it is also ideal when the project leader is really excited about the task at hand.

Of course, for the IT-Vision-Tour, there was also a project leader, and that was my position. I was so excited about this idea that I affected all of the others with my passion. At the same time, we all had (in addition to euphoria) a concrete time and plan including weekly team calls on the status, open questions, and additional ideas. Each person on the close-knit team (the individual employees as well as the partners) was asked to deliver intermediate data within a predefined deadline.

It is always good to have one person really concentrating on holding the partnership together, even if it is just when working on a small project. This is why many software companies have partner managers. It is also advisable to contractually regulate the cooperation between partners because, as time passes, the employees responsible for and trusted with the information of the partnership may also change. If you have the particulars of a cooperation on black and white, you will always have a good base to build upon, even with changing teams.

Eight Tips for a Functioning Partnership
- Define the exact goals of your new partnership. While doing so, also define your common target groups.
- Pay attention to concepts and methods that create a win-win situation for both. Every partnership thrives when both partners profit.
- Collaborative marketing activities expand the marketable universe and collective sales activities make the market penetration easier. It is important that your company cooperates with the partner company in the different functional departments.
- The customer should also profit from the partnership. It is very important that the customer can recognize the value of the partnership.
- Be conscious of the fact that a partnership is also a business obligation and behave loyally and accordingly.
- Every partnership wants to be built and cared for like a business relationship, so be prepared to invest time and resources.
- It is very important to understand the goals and expectations of your partner before you enter into the first activity together. Make sure you plan enough time to thoroughly discuss goals or participate in a workshop together. Look at all aspects of the partner company, including the important decision makers on each side.
- Set common milestones so that you can measure the intermediate success and correct any problems for the future / moving forward.

"Taking on the Full Risk – for Only Half of the Success?"

By Gabriele Rittinghaus

The question in the title is no serious argument against a business partnership. I am a firm believer that a partnership can enable and ensure the survival of one or both partners. There are, however, some aspects to take into consideration. This is true for both the selection of partners, as well as the implementation of a commonly defined goal.

- Why is a company seeking a partnership – for which reasons?
- It wants to achieve particular marketing or sales goals and in doing so, profit from the strengths of the partner.
- It wants to dominate the market power together with a competitor.
- It wants to enhance individual strategic strengths, especially compensating for weaknesses, in order to achieve quick and secure access to a new market.

There are a variety of different partnerships that can also strongly diverge from one another in their connection.

Sales Partnership: the mutual use of a distribution channel. With this cooperation, the partners can use new sales channels, in order to expand their target market through the integration of both of their current channels. On the other side, through the incorporation of the services of the partners, the customer can expect an increased product offering and therefore more added value and use is offered. In addition, through cooperation in sales, new target groups can be addressed more easily, since the already existing customers of the partners have been solicited.

For example, in cooperation with the bank comdirect, Tchibo (a German chain of coffee shops and cafes who are also known for their weekly-changing range of other household products) offered customers on its online shop a variety of financial savings products like savings accounts and various bond options.

Product Bundling: combined and time limited offerings of one or two products in a packet for one price. Cooperation in the form of a product bundle targets a quicker sales approach during the product introduction phase, a stronger competitive edge, the use of synergy effects, as wells as the increase in sales numbers, above all. In addition, an increase in sales from a product with less inquires, can be achieved through product bundling.

For example: Microsoft and almost every hardware manufacturer. The hardware company delivers its hardware already equipped with Microsoft Office as a standard – and Microsoft can continue to build upon its monopolizing position.

Marketing Collaboration: the cooperation between at least two marketing organizations with the goal of tapping into the market potential, through the bundling of specific components or resources. The value of the end customer is in the forefront for both partners. The company recognizes an approach to the achievement of a growth potential, which they could not achieve on their own, due to the fact that they lack certain competencies. Furthermore, a marketing collaboration can offer a more flexible, efficient and short term possibility for a common growth for both partners.

For example, Unilever's ice cream brand "Cremissimo" cooperates with many famous food companies like Milka, Toblerone, and Batida de Coco, to position themselves against the competition and react quicker to the newest trends. One month after the start of the Milka Cremissimo campaign and it already became the most sold ice cream on the German market.

Strategic Alliance: A close collaboration between many companies and their even closer and most significant business partners. This partnership may exist in secret or it may be openly advertised.

Many examples of this alliance are from the automobile industry. They conduct common development activities for automobile components and almost every car manufacturer does this.

Strategic alliances can also go further, as the following example shows: Daimler and Renault have decided to create a cross-over cooperation in the form of a mutual contribution of capital. Together they will develop smaller cars.

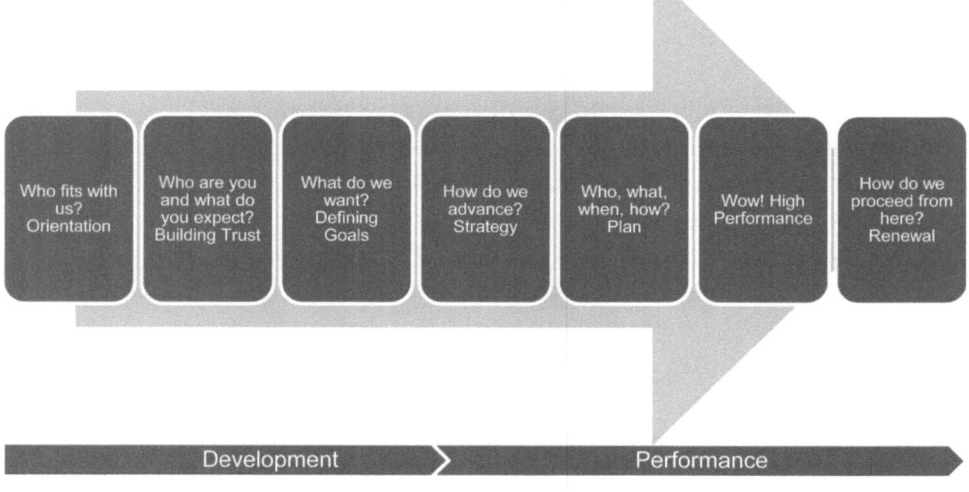

The Seven Phases of a Business Partnership

"Taking on the Full Risk – for Only Half of the Success?"

The "Welt AG" from the former Daimler boss, Jürgen Schremp, was completed when Mitsubishi from Japan made a joint venture, creating a marriage made in heaven – a triangular relationship between them, Mercedes and Chrysler.

Regardless of which of these above-listed partnerships that you choose to undertake, the success of the business model relies on motivation of both of the partners. Unclear expectations, different interfaces, insufficiently defined tasks and duties can slow and irritate the process of the partnership. There are many "soft factors" that can lead to disagreements. The scale and scope of a collaboration must be discussed in detail.

An increase in efficiency and a reduction in costs can be achieved through collective marketing activities and mutual use of the sales and logistic structures. Customer's orders can be worked on together and to do so, every participant must fulfill their previously defined task.

The trick is to choose a partner who can deliver exactly what you are missing. Both partners must fulfill the requirements that are necessary for a functioning business. In addition, both partners must vigorous in their wish for this partnership to succeed – and also they must be therefore so excited to have found the right partner.

When goals and the general conditions are not commonly and amicably agreed upon, either the cooperation will not produce the desired results or the tasks of each partner could clash, which can have the potential to lead to conflict.

Therefore, take a note from Goethe:

"Being successful needs two things: clear goals and the burning desire to achieve them."

Selecting and motivating employees
Creating the ideal team

There is nothing more valuable for a company then having employees that are as motivated as qualified.

Just simply having a lot of individually good employees do not create success. One needs a perfect team. A group that has different character traits: one that harmonizes and where its colleagues are loyal and can trust one another.

Motivation is the drive to succeed in every team, even in the work environment.

This is an eminent criterion, especially in times of small teams and mini budgets. However, great motivation will not come by itself. The team leader is responsible for encouraging and stipulating the motivation from the team members. Therefore, the team leader needs to possess intuition about his or her team members, the ability to empathize and he or she also needs tremendous communication skill. Celebrating success and creating development opportunities – from advanced trainings to externally moderated workshops to conventions – these are just small add-ons in this subject matter. Most importantly is the correct communication. This is where the boss is very important. He or she must make the decisions transparent for the employees and must inform them about strategies and goals. If the manager does not explain enough or expect too much they often run the risk of falling into the communications trap. This is when an employee knows less than the boss thinks that he or she really knows. In this situation the employee ends up making a mistake by overlooking detail or is unmotivated since he or she do not understand what the boss is asking for.

Talking is silver and listening is gold

The manager should not always talk and inform. He or she needs to listen.

For example, if an employee presents a new solutions on how to approach solving a problem for an ongoing project. Employees are usually a lot more involved with much more in depth details of a case then their boss is. Employees have information that their boss does not (yet) have. In this case the manager's idea diverges from its employee. But in this case the boss should listen for the motives and reasons that the employee is presenting. Maybe the employee is correct with his or her deliberations. It is also important that the boss will make an open approach on to the employee's character. This works if one listens and empathizes. This is the only way a person potential can be detected and fostered.

Growing the potential of employees also requires that they are given their need freedom. That is why, whenever it getting exciting, I do not put on the brakes (where ever it is possible). This in turn motivates each and every one, to work self-responsible and think entrepreneurial. In short: I prefer a macro management approach, in which I set great guidelines, but leave a lot of freedom to my employees and do not interfere in their day to day business. This is exactly how professional employees get motivated. Anything else would only impair their dedication

> **Seven Tips for Forming your Dream Team:**
> - It's up to you to form the team – and to keep it in shape
> - Communicate regularly with your team and more importantly, with each member. Introduce projects to the team in a way that everyone really understands and so that they know why and how they should approach them
> - Listen carefully

- Motivate your team to innovative thinking and acting. Be loyal to your team and let them know that they can depend on you.
- Show your team that you are invested in them. Implement team building activities.
- Demanding and delivering go together: recognize talent and develop each individual.
- Present and celebrate success

You should nit-pick: the job advertisements

There is always a person who fits the job, you just have to find them. Therefore you have to make it clear, what skills the new person must have, what they must be able to do, and what they have to accomplish, as well as what the position requires. Then a precise job description practically creates itself. Only when you have the answers to these questions, can you begin looking for the candidate. You can only obtain a decent selection of people if you have a clear advertisement that states exactly what you are looking for. This helps human resources secure talented candidates for the first interview and therefore the entire hiring process is more goal oriented and efficient.

Choosing an employee is not speed dating

I recommend big companies to hold six to eight interviews with the job applicant to really be able to estimate him. Only then will the interviewers have a fundamental impression. Small companies should also invest time in the selection of their employees. In this case, decisions made in error can lead to lack of performance and in the worst case, consequential costs, when it comes out that the selected candidate is not the right one for the job.

As a rule, I normally hold interviews with a colleague from

the team. It is also worthwhile to have the candidate speak with the sales manager or another colleague from a different department. This gives the candidate a new perspective on the company and gives the company a second opinion on the candidate. In the end, the hiring process can take between two to three weeks. I also recommend not to book more than two interviews per day for the candidate.

When all the interviews are done and all of the questions have been asked, and you are still not 100% sure, speaking with former managers and colleagues for references can help. You can also have the potential employee work for two to three days as a test run. That is one way to obtain a clear view of the candidate. We used this tactic on one of our candidates and it was evident that even though he was highly qualified, he was unable to handle the pressure that the job demanded. Finding this out in advance was a win for both sides. The team and the applicant both avoided making an error in judgment and the extremely competent candidate increased his chance of becoming the right one for another position.

Wanted: Someone with Guts!

What does the ideal team member look like? He should be qualified, innovative, cooperative, honest, respectful, tolerant and of course, enthusiastic. He is passionate about his job. This should be true for new assistants as well as new managers. Lastly, they should think entrepreneurially, they should be self-confident and trust themselves to go in a new direction.

It sounds like when you find this person, you are guaranteed to have a successful business. But unfortunately, we live in hard times for creative, outside-the-box thinkers. The financial crisis and lay-offs in 2009 lead to many workers being more cautious, out of fear for losing their valuable job. A dilemma, for when resources are low, we need people with guts and original ideas.

> "the best thing a manager can do is hire the right people." –
> Lee Iacocca

Dry Runs

We know now how the ideal candidate for a described position looks. So how can we recognize them if they are sitting before us? My opinion is that the good old case study helps. It is the most classic and probably most efficient method to learn more about the candidate and their way of working. I give the job applicant a case study from experience and see what kind of answers they come up with. Normally, this gives me a variety of knowledge. For example, I once asked a candidate to create a marketing concept for the fictional creation of a garden center in Ikea, with all of the classic marketing tools and a limited budget. After one day of preparation, she presented me with such a convincing concept that we didn't just hire her, but we also adapted some of her ideas for marketing our company.

Of course only a few applicants can do this easily. Very seldom are you so convinced of one idea, that you ignore alternative proposals. And that is good so, for the question of different approaches also tests the candidates. This will show whether or not he is flexible enough to throw out his first ideas and develop a new, even better one. This is an ability that a marketing professional should have.

In the interview setting, you can find out how enthusiastic a candidate is. Does he speak with enjoyment about the ideas and projects? Or is this just a part of his job, for him? Does he speak in the first person singular or plural – is he not just engaged, but also team oriented? Whoever listens closely can find out a lot about the candidate. Under most circumstances, you can find out what type of worker he is: strategic, theoretic, converter or do-er? Which roll he will play in the future is good to know, so that the team can also adjust to his entry and stay evenly proportioned.

Recruiting Outside the Box

There are tons of brilliant marketing and sales managers in the IT branch, that are the masters of their tools. However, in the course of the last few years, there has been an industry standard that is only broken every once in a while.

Therefore, in my company, we value the input from industry newcomers and we like to recruit outside of the box. Sometimes we fill a channel position with someone from the automobile industry. For an event management position, we often fill it with someone who has hotel experience. They have organizational talent, are reliable, know how to work with a small budget and know what is required from them on a service level. In addition, they value the advantages that our branch offers: no working in shifts, better pay, and an environment with development opportunities.

Seven Tips for a Successful Staff Search
- The more precise the job description, the better the chances of receiving a good selection of candidates
- Talk with the human resources department or the recruiter about your expectations, since these people are the first point of contact with your candidates and can filter them accordingly
- Ask your colleagues who are qualified if they know anyone who would be interested in the position. The saying is true – "good people know good people"- and maybe they can recommend an interesting candidate to you.
- Take people from other industries and departments into consideration
- Listen well: especially in the interview. Listen to what is not being said and observe the voice, tone and gestures of the candidate. My opinion is that the former often tells more about the person than their words.

> - Speak with their former managers and colleagues. In contrast with before, some certificates are not enough.
> - The team should also help to decide. In the end, the new person will also be part of the team. The future colleagues should also be able to voice their opinion on the candidate. That way both sides can get an impression of one another.

Everything Depends on the Type

"A person can never be perfect, but a team could be." According to this, every individual in a team is an important piece of the puzzle. And this puzzle should ideally be composed of different but complementing people who integrate and work well together.

The Team Management System (TMS) from Charles Margerison and Dick McCann shows the different types of people who should be found in teams. Even if when I support this concept completely and recognize that I need all types in the team, it's obvious to me that some types are more important than others when it comes to innovation. The Do-er, the Strategist, the Theorist, and the Translator, as I call them.

The Do-er lives in the here and now. He is concrete, calls for action on the points, and gives the team members clear instructions. As a driven person, he loves to move things and set an example. He is constantly looking for change and for improvement possibilities. When things don't move quickly enough, he gets impatient and can stimulate the entire team – in a positive way. All in all, he is not afraid to take risks and is therefore, a very important element of the team.

The Strategist has his vision (the big picture) on his radar. He doesn't lose himself in tactical deliberations, but rather describes his vision mostly on an abstract level. Quite often, he may need a translator, to deliver these visionary ideas to the team and takes care that the idea can be comprehensively directed. The visionary thinks about the middle to long term future and can't understand how someone can lose themselves in the present.

The Theorist is the big future planner. He takes his ideas from the present and with small, measured steps, he develops tomorrow from today. As a rule, the theorist is conscious and close to reality, however now and then, they may lose their objectivity.

The Translator, on the other hand, doesn't get anything from concentrating on the upcoming year or any further. He wants clear and direct instructions for this week, month or quarter. Then he can really get started. Pragmatic and without a doubt on the task at hand. The result, what pays for him, is that he fulfills the tasks and then he is on to the next one. If you want to achieve results, the translator is the perfect addition to the team.

The Who's Who in the Team

In order to estimate the talent, abilities, aptitudes and passions of the individual team members, Margerison and McCann have developed a framework to measure their characteristics, strategic approach to problems, general work behavior, ability to handle stress, work preferences and communication skills.

The answers classify each person on the team and can offer you an evaluation of which type they correspond with. These classifications are also helpful when it comes to selecting candidates, because it shows the employer which role they would most likely assume on the team.

Evaluating employees based on their type qualifications is not a science – people grow as their tasks change. I could also notice a change over the years in myself. In terms of the type categories, I was first a Translator, then a Do-er, and now I am a Strategist. I can now associate this metamorphosis with my career jumps. Although regardless of the changes, I could still consider myself the translator – even today.

The Boss as a Coach

Trust can only flourish on with a foundation of reciprocity" –
ALBERT EINSTEIN

Even the very best team cannot achieve their goals if the manager is not fulfilling his position correctly. Above all, his main task is to push the team to deliver more and cultivate them at the same time. Is there an issue with our technical knowledge or is the problem existing on a personal level? A good manager can identify the issue and handles it. Either by coaching the employees himself (when he has the training to do so properly) or by obtaining external advice.

If the relationship between the manager and the employee is particularly collegial, and perhaps the employee only wishes to discuss things amongst someone he can trust, then perhaps the manager is the appropriate coach. But if the relationship is a little bit distanced or a certain discrepancy is involved, then it is better to get help from outside the organization. Also, if the employee knows that he or she needs a less familiar relationship, in order to accept the advice, than this is a strong argument for outside help. In either case, both sides should agree to the tactic, and the employee should feel well justified. That is the most important requirement for positive coaching.

The same is true for coaching, for that matter: whoever is prepared to take on the role of the coach, should also be able to put himself in the place of the employee. Only once a person is able to do this, can they really produce meaningful answers. In the process, the coach is not giving the answers but rather helping the employee to develop an answer himself.

As a manager, you find yourself often in the position of the coach, even if you are not specially trained for this. Admittedly, there are always more and more superiors who possess natural talent, but a certain methodical knowledge is always advisable. An additional training or advance course will always help if you are taking on more personnel responsibilities over the course of time. I myself have completed an intensive course on coaching and can only recommend this. Rarely have I done anything more exciting!

The Inner Solidarity

"Die Treue" – German for loyalty, describes an inner solidarity and the effect it has on your behavior with others, groups, and your community. Loyalty is believing in the value of another person and being an advocate for them, even when they do not share in the advocacy themselves. Loyalty is always a voluntary matter. It is demonstrated not just by your behavior to the one whom you are loyally connected, but also by third parties. That is the theory and we can deduce many things from actual practice, such as the knowledge that a common and mutual loyalty between a manager and his employees is the best basis for a successful cooperation. This means that a manager and his employees can depend on one another.

On this common ground of mutual trust, you are not just able to work efficiently, but it also becomes fun to know that you can build upon each other's strengths. The loyalty between a manager and employees is neither guaranteed nor is it there from the beginning. You have to successfully develop it and let it ripen over time. How long it takes is dependent on the personal situation. About a year is what you can normally expect.

Work Together, Talk Together

Many team problems exist, because people did not talk to one another or there where many misunderstandings or miscommunications. I remember a conflict with one colleague who tried to ignore the guidelines I have set and just did his own thing. Of course, I was especially upset because I found this behavior to be disloyal. I thought that I informed the employee of his guidelines in detail and I couldn't understand his behavior. However, when we spoke, I learned that he was missing information and he didn't know exactly what I wanted and why. Apparently, I did not brief him well enough and he misinterpreted the missing details and built his own opinion of the situation, bringing my decision into question. On the other hand, I assumed his actions demonstrated a lack of loyalty. In the end, it was a typical misunderstanding due to lack of communication, which is the most common reason for disagreements between managers and their employees.

As I realized that a lack of communication on my side had caused this conflict, I apologized for my mistake and learned something for the future. Since then, I present my ideas in more detail and only after I have thought through everything. Above all, I occupy myself with the concept that as soon as I understand a topic fully, I explain it to the others in detail so that they understand exactly why we approach the project in one particular way and not in a different way. I got that message (from my mistake), that people think differently, and that when I have come to terms with my ideas in my own head, it is not always comprehensible for others.

In addition, I learned from this incident to always try to be on the offense and have a clear talk. This can lead to pleasant turnarounds and "a-ha!" moments quite frequently.

Cooperatively Close Instead of Neutrally Distant

Some employees (and colleagues) are convinced that they can only be respectful employees if they behave in a way that is neutral and distanced. This is not a proven fact. Quite often, it is shown that you can give up much when you are distanced, namely, intensive personal exchanges, fire-and-flame discussion, and perhaps new ideas.

My opinion is that a person can absolutely avoid distancing themselves on all hierarchical levels and, if they are able to do so, managers and employees alike will find that cooperation becomes more lively and exciting. I believe that it is the manager's responsibility to provide for more collegial closeness.

It is especially important to approach the more introverted employees. Not everyone can and will be outgoing. Often additional attention and good natured interest can suffice to bring these people out of their reserve and help them to relax. This also helps to promote their abilities, depending on how they are, and helps reveal them to others.

Showtime for the Employee

Humans are vain creatures and, as such, they need admiration every once in a while. This positive regeneration can lead to new heights. Therefore, this can be deduced for the professional life: an employee should be able to present themselves and what they can offer and should not shy away from the limelight. Only he who can present what he has achieved to others will directly receive the motivating recognition from his manager and colleagues.

Therefore, even the introverted contemporaries should take the leap into the limelight. Only there they will learn how to present themselves and their ideas in the right fashion and experience how positive feedback can make you more confident, and they may work up the courage to go on stage more often.

One of my colleagues had this experience a few years ago. She was very technically competent and had an enormous amount of detailed knowledge. What she lacked was trust in herself and in her ability to present her compelling ideas to the team, so she avoided giving presentations to the team and avoided showing her very good work results. A dream for every manager is to be able to present a team success as their own. This was never my dream, because I want confident employees. Through some coaching, she overcame her shyness and trained herself to present in small groups at first and then larger ones later. Slowly, she grew more secure, her ambition was awakened, and she was more confident in front of a large group. Today, she is a marketing expert, who is sought out for her professional presentations that attract large groups of people.

Normal Working Times, in Normal Times

At the end of the working day, there has to be an end – that's how I handle things with my employees. I don't require (and also don't forbid) that they show their presence especially long. I think that in normal work situations, an employee should be able to finish his or her work load within the normal workday time. However, if we are in a particularly stressful time, it is clear that we have to work together (just like during normal work situations) until project is finished. This is a requirement that is not often questioned during normal work situations and is still a requirement under stressful conditions.

I am a firm believer: no marketing manager in the world has to be available 24/7, 365 days a year and shouldn't regularly be spending long nights in the office. Whoever dictates these kinds of hours to their employees should ask themselves whether or not this organizational structure is really necessary. If he doesn't do this, he will constantly lose good employees. Everyone needs a rejuvenation period, when they can refuel and gain new energy, and good employees know this!

> ### Seven Do's for Employee Management
> - Practice Macromanagement. Micromanagement may work for junior managers, but definitely not when you are working with more experienced employees. You can't expect senior management and then control everything in detail.
> - Inform extensively. Incomplete information or weak objectives can confuse the team. State what you want to achieve clearly and concisely.

- Manage consistently. Changing your mind or direction can disorient, therefore, you should stick to your decisions.
- Allow freedom of decision in moderation. Your employees should have as much freedom to decide as possible, but too much freedom can mean jeopardizing a project. The best way is to start with small projects with a lot of self-reliance and give successively more responsibility after successful implementation.
- Never loosen the reins. You are responsible for the team and their success. In every instance, you should have an entire overview of the project and know (maybe even in detail) how each aspect is functioning.
- Don't let anything become private. Everyone's private and professional life should always be a bit distanced. That doesn't mean that colleagues can't become friends. However, it is always best when a professional distance exists.
- Don't allow any disloyalty. If an employee is acting disloyally in your eyes, clear up the situation immediately. If it involves the team, make your position clear to the team after the problem has been solved.

"Diversity of Innovative Factors"
By Torsten Bittlingmaier

Of course there are those who are especially innovative – the Thomas Jeffersons of the world, who are brimming with ideas and define themselves by the amount of inventions in a day – but these people are an exception. In daily business, innovation is often difficult work. Although many inventions were discovered on accident in the past, some factors are easily recognized that can promote the creative of innovation.

In addition to intrinsic motivation and individual attributes of a person – for example, his or her curiosity, perseverance, engagement, and willingness to take risks – underlying conditions that are consciously created play a role and can have an effect on the success factors for innovation.

The factors which you should examine closely are diversity, learning in networks, and room for innovation.

Aspects of diversity

Diversity has many facets; a main emphasis is placed on the classic elements of modern diversity: Gender, international mixture, and age heterogeneity.

Diversity

The fact that groups achieve better results and are more innovative than an individual is no new knowledge. Anyone that has played the famous game NASA (look up Klaus Anton's "Practice of Group Dynamics", Hogrefe Publishing, Göttingen 2000) can experience the impressive influence of a group.

Additional potential lies in the consistency of the

group. The Phoenix Report, from the consulting group Accenture, leaves no doubt that mixed teams record better results than homogenous teams. Other studies also prove this. For example, a McKinsey study from 2007 that showed that businesses with a high percentage of women on the board of directors have achieved significantly better financial figures than companies with less women on the board (including return on sales, return on equity, and return on invested capital).

The theme of gender is gaining more and more meaning. A chief executive named Kasper Rorstedt from the company Henkel, was quoted in a financial journal as saying this about the previously named study: "Our diversity is our industrial strength". That message is very clear to us – we want more women in executive positions. The German Telekom made an even more impressive move: they have enacted a quota for women and want at least 30% of executive and middle management positions filled by women by the year 2015. Motto: "Success through diversity."

What's more is that internationally assembled teams reach better decisions, especially about foreign markets. This development is already evident in the composition of the board of directors of the DAX companies. Just counting the CEO's, we can find a Swedish person, an Austrian, a Swiss, etc. This is no coincidence, but rather proof of the knowledge that global or internationally engaged companies that wish to be innovative and successful, need to ensure that their executives are internationally diverse.

Although this is not yet visible on an executive level, there is still another aspect of diversity in work groups that is increasingly valued: diversity of ages. What's becoming more common is that teams are knowingly creating a structure where experienced employees and rookies who possess current knowledge from their education are paired together. Considering the waning half-life of IT knowledge (half of the current IT knowledge will lose its meaning within two years) has made this clear – the acceptance of available knowledge explains why the reverse-mentoring concept (where experienced employees are educated by their younger counterparts) is no longer made fun of and has become an accepted success factor of innovation and knowledge management. Modern management teams are therefore diverse and profit from the experience of multiple generations. Stephen R. Covey defines maturity as the balance between guts and consideration, in his book "The Seven Ways to Effectiveness" (Gabal Publishers, Offenbach 2010). Balanced teams can achieve a higher level of maturity and can contribute to the good of the company.

Different Branches

In addition to the classic diversity criteria, there are more aspects to consider when assembling a team.

Benchmarking is believed to be a method of goal-oriented comparisons that lead to an optimization of processes, products, etc. and often involves functioning interdepartmental approaches. An analogy to this would be the benefits received when a team from one side has the industry-specific knowledge available but they call in employees with experience from other industries. From my own experience, I can report how a change of industry can be enriching from both a personal and professional standpoint. The ability to scrutinize the professional structures and processes as a newbie is a valuable source of innovation. Unfortunately, this can dry up after some time and the assimilation begins...

We all know the theory that with the increasing responsibility of a position in a hierarchy, the required know-how from the correspondent person decreases while the ability to manage things, however, becomes more important. We find examples for this in the corporate world, especially in politics, where a department change for a minister is common practice.

Changing departments offers you the chance to train your abstraction ability. The existence of this ability in a team, paired with enough traction, is a good basis for innovative thinking and acting. Getting people who think outside of the box is not always easy. In competitive times, these people might fall through the cracks of your screening process. People looking to change industries are often a really good compromise. They are already able to prove their professionalism, they can fulfill the requirements of the job profile, and they are able to enrich the team with new experience and perspectives. Remind yourself: industry-specific knowledge often has a formidable reputation but is not always as useful as it may seem. Do any business examples come to your mind? Wolfgang Reitzle was a successful automobile company manager and then became an even more successful CEO of the industrial gas company, The Linde Group. Eckhard Cordes, also from the automobile industry, works today as the chief executive of the Metro Group. Peter Löscher came from Kienbaum (consulting), Hoechst and Aventis (chemistry), General Electric (healthcare), and Merck (pharmaceuticals) to Siemens and is today the chief executive of the board of directors. Are these all exceptions to the rule? Surely not. More like *the* rule – an ever increasing tendency.

Learning in Networks

Learning has a lot to do with innovation... that makes sense. If you ask the question about whether the education models today are promoting innovation, an honest answer (even in the best case) would have to be a resounding 'only partly'.

Also, in view of new developments regarding value change and web 2.0 technologies, we have to ask ourselves how the leaders and employees of the future will learn, especially within the perspective of the innovation that will be required from them.

The theme of cross hierarchical learning is here quintessential. Normally, leading executives meet one another at executive seminars and build a dependable network – sometimes this is supported through corresponding alumni meetings. This will also be required in the future, however, this will only achieve its purpose if the meetings and networks are independent from hierarchies.

Example A – the classic: The executives have developed a new technique or instrument in a seminar and would like to integrate this into their everyday workplace. The employees, who were not involved and did not execute this, react with incomprehension or rejections. Innovational fail.

Example B – The modern version: Executives and employees learn these new techniques together in a seminar and work together to integrate these into the daily business of the company. Any oppositions can be worked out in the seminar. The result is real innovation and a mutual advancement to a new level of development.

Innovation Needs Space

An obvious truth, but still not minded in cases of doubt. Space is not meant in the literal sense, but above all the necessary space of time. Often times we clear space for operative topics more than strategic, but innovation also involves strategy. The classic positive example comes from 3M, where they allow their employees to dedicate 15% of their work time to their own projects and ideas. From that time, for example, Post-It notes were developed.

The ability and the opportunity to reflect builds an excellent base for innovation. The task is therefore to consciously and often create the opportunity of time, in which reflection and space is given to innovation. This can be a walk through the woods or fields, an engaging discussion with friends or colleagues, a visit to conventions or lectures, or simply switching off your smartphone.

By the way, when the famous German show, "Wetten, dass …" first went on the air in February 1981, it was also an experiment in Saturday night television entertainment. It is said that Frank Elstner, the founder of the show, had dreamed about the idea of this show in his sleep. Perhaps Frank was in a lucky position, to use his sleep as time for the development of innovation.

Innovation in a Circle

At first look, it seems incomprehensible that innovational leaps can be observed even in times of crisis, and that's when the Phoenix Effect, as described by Regina Mehler, goes into effect. Through closer examination, one can conclude that innovation is actually enabled in times of crisis, because:

- There is a higher pressure for change
- The willingness to take a different path increases
- There is an increased readiness to make personnel and organizational changes
- Often teams are built outside of the organization as tasks forces – and these are commonly heterogeneous but they are at least cross-functional
- The executional probability of unconventional ideas increases

Innovation isn't just created; it is actually followed through with a higher probability than normal. Charles Darwin already described this principle to some effect when he said that neither the strong nor the intelligent are the ones who survive, but rather those who are in the best position to adapt to changes. Does an example from today's business world come to mind? Take a look at the development of the company Lanxess: they evolved from a random collection of companies so far in deficient that the Bayer-Konzern did not want any more to a "special chemistry provider, with new brands, technological leadership and globality"(Axel Heitmann, chief executive of the Lanxess Group in managermagazin, July 2010)

Innovational Strategy

According to Klaus Doppler, consultant and change management expert, innovation is the twin sister of adaptation. This can't be simply prescribed, but must be able to be developed.

Many factors enable innovation and we have discussed some of them previously. A deciding factor is that the topic of innovation is regarded as a strategic, competitive edge that is systematically executed and is consequent on the company's general framework, enabling those to work on innovational abilities.

If we believe that more women in executive positions and more international participation in deciding teams means that it creates more diversity and more overall motivation to innovation, then the following underlying conditions must be established: part-time management, flexible working times, ability to work from home, or to work virtually with a convenient mixture of team time and time to reflect, just as an example.

The strategy of strengthening teams with more of the same is a local minded tendency – it has no place in our globalized world.

Mutual Goals, Mutual Success

Alignment – the ideal cooperation between marketing and sales

> "The only goal of marketing is to make sales redundant. The goal of marketing is to understand the customer and his needs, so that the developed product fits them so well that it can sell itself." –
>
> PETER F. DRUCKER

Due to the financial crisis of 2008, the project business in the software industry changed (and probably in many other industries as well). Before, many projects in the enterprise business were negotiated. Today many small projects are started in a series, beginning with a pilot project first. The pilot's process is critically followed by the customer and then when it is really running well, then they think about the next steps.

Also, in regards to the results, the customer has become more demanding. He doesn't want to sell software or solutions. He wants to see concrete value for his business – and preferably right after the project begins.

In short, the decision makers became more challenging and more careful. They have to manage with smaller budgets and are under pressure more than before. Therefore, they spend their money in smaller increments and make sure that they invest it well.

That's how the sale of software and many other products has become more complex. As a result, not only does the sales department have to rethink their strategies, but the marketing team does too – including the sales processes with smaller parts, which, as a rule, have more people involved in the decision making process. Therefore, the campaigns have to be more strongly segmented and tailored to more target groups. This is, of course, correlated with a higher cost.

At the same time as the crisis, not only were the IT budgets cut, but so were the marketing budgets and the teams. More work with less people and less budget: this means that the marketing teams and other departments found themselves in the same boat.

More efficiency is asked from marketing. Every campaign

must bring in the optimal results, since the money is carefully measured for each offer. In order for the campaign to achieve its potential, marketing has to endeavor to be close to the customers and know exactly what they want. Only then can the campaign team and their ambassadors, the messaging, coordinate optimally to the target group.

In order for it to work, marketing requires substantial information about the customers. What are their needs? Which special interests? What did they buy in the past? On which aspects do they base their buying decisions? With all of these questions and their answers, Customer Relationship Management (CRM) and Business Information (BI) have experienced a boom. Not just in the software industry, but also in every telecommunications business, every insurance company, and every online store or shop. Just take a look at the client cards you have in your wallet – they describe your consumer behavior. Haven't you noticed how many emails Amazon send you due to the fact that your purchases show what your tastes in books and music are?

CRM and BI are just some of many different possibilities for collecting information about the client, but for us marketers in a complex IT enterprise business, this does not suffice, for our task is to understand the complex businesses of our customers and their need for support through software solutions. This cannot be summarized with sparse information. Instead, we in enterprise marketing are asked and challenged to build a fundamental understanding of the issues our customers face. And this occurs only with a tight cooperation with the customer and with sales.

When short and long no longer work together

Nothing is closer to the cooperation between marketing and sales, who both inform each other about what the client needs, how to reach them, and with which method to approach them. However, in many companies, cooperation between sales and marketing is not always guaranteed. Quite the opposite – sometimes the employees from both departments work against each other and sometimes there is even a tradition of disagreement.

The reason for such lies in the fact that they lack understanding of one another and this lack of understanding is due to the fact that they don't speak often enough with each other. An additional potential conflict between marketing and sales could be that they have different planning horizontals: even though the sales cycle of big projects can take many months, even a year, sales is more oriented around quarters. Accordingly, they try to bring in quick profits at the end of the quarter. In summary, a sales team thinks in more short term, end-of-the-quarter figures, while marketing plans for more long term results.

The task of marketing is to cultivate interest and attention for a company or a product and, from that, generate an ever-increasing demand. This requires a deep engagement as well as long term, strategic thinking. Potentially, marketing concepts should be well-analyzed. This can lead to conflicts more often. For example, sales would like a quick marketing offer in order to achieve their target revenue by the end of the quarter however, the long term thinking people on the marketing team do not want to invest any money in this. Or, sales would like to (quickly) reach out to a new target group. Marketing agrees, but they prefer to have a solid concept and analysis, which takes too long for the impatient sales team. They question why we need so long and what marketing really does the whole time.

It can also be complicated when the marketing team develops complex campaigns without checking them with sales in advance. If sales doesn't understand the messaging of the campaign or they think it won't work and they doubt the campaign content, the marketing offer may not work properly.

Instead of going with "one voice to the market", the campaign can amount to nothing, for if the customer receives an email, video, or brochure with messaging that doesn't come from sales, then the solution or product that you are trying to promote will not be convincing. As a rule, many campaigns end with such confusion from all sides.

Often times, the sales team has the prejudice that the marketing team just has the ladies who order the snacks for events and hand out the newest product brochures. This is a misconception that the marketing manager or director must address before he or she can work successfully.

Preconceptions, misunderstandings, or conflicts – just like in other areas of life – can be avoided by continually working together and exchanging information. Marketing and sales can respectively inform each other about the goals, plans, and activities from each other so that they can think and act together. Then, they are able to generate revenue together. Above everything, it is important for marketing to use the know-how from the sales team. Sales knows how the customer ticks and what they need, and therefore they are a useful source of information, but marketing shouldn't just use sales as a pure information giver. Alternatively, they are obligated to inform sales about offers, campaigns, knowledge and the results of marketing analysis and customer feedback.

Partner Practice

An ideal cooperation between marketing and sales looks like this: at the beginning of each year, the two departments sit together and define which markets to address with which products and exactly which goals they would like to achieve together. This is the basis of every go-to-market plan. Markets, products, and revenue goals are defined and the marketing team conceptualizes the content and strategic approach. When this is successfully outlined, the next meeting occurs to get alignment from all sides. When marketing gets the go ahead, the next step is the definition of the positioning. (In case of a no-go, the process begins from the start).

When the content of the next actions are laid out, there must be another round of approval. At this level can the potential test round begin; the messaging in sales – namely, the sales approach, can be tested live with the customer. This may not be possible with large campaigns, because no one wants communicate a campaign in advance with the customer that may run for many months or quarters. The first feedback from a customer is very important for the marketing team because it demonstrates whether or not that messaging works properly.

Tests like this allow marketing to modify certain campaigns early enough and actually make the adjustments that are needed. Only then can sales get what they want: a campaign that speaks to the customer and can generate a lot of demand for the product.

When the customer understands the messaging and feels like it speaks to them, marketing can begin fine-tuning the content and graphics. Parallel to this, sales enablement tools should be developed with the product manager or the business development manager. Sales enablement material is content that launches the campaign to all sales employees, or better yet – all company employees – and informs everyone that this campaign is available and what purpose it serves. These enablement tools help employees to properly communicate the campaign in their environment.

The Enablement Package should include a customer presentation and paperwork that explains which goals the campaign wants to achieve and which messaging should be used for each target group. This package serves to explain the campaign and generate excitement among employees. The sales enablement process is just as important as the campaign itself.

Get Out of the Ivory Tower

Cooperation with sales is the first step to getting closer to the market. The second way works more directly – speaking with the customers.

That's why marketing managers should regularly visit clients with the sales team. Only through personal discussions can one really get an idea of what the situation is and what the customer's needs are. A marketing manager who never participated in a customer discussion is just a theorist, and would find it difficult to develop messaging that touches the customer. Even when marketing and sales cooperate closely together, without direct customer contact, it's like you are in the Ivory Tower. It is a real difference if you know first-hand which questions are applicable to the customer, what moves them, and with which topics they are concerned. Only with direct contact can you get a feel for what the customer needs and how you can help them find a solution to their problems.

In talks with the customers, you can also experience how much he knows about your product portfolio and your company and which information he is lacking. You also find out how sales has positioned your company and products and how they have approached the needs of the customer so that you can better support them. In the best (or worst) case scenario in a customer discussion, a marketer can learn whether or not we have addressed the customer's needs with our communication.

If you are a marketer who does not speak with the client, you are like a cross country skier who trains on roller skates in the summer – you have the concept and the technique, but you are lacking a real feel for true cross country skiing, on real skis, in real snow when it is cold.

I personally am always looking for the opportunity to speak with customers. It is also important to me to meet my contact not just once, but many times, because, of course, every meeting brings new knowledge and increases my understanding of the situation of my customer. This is not just true for a sales discussion. It is also just as interesting to listen in on a case study interview or exchange information with the customer in the course of a new event. Both offer new perspectives and can bring other aspects of the situation to light.

Fish Campaigns

"The worm must taste good to the fish and not to the fisher."
This saying is a bit outdated but is still meaningful. Sometimes, marketers fall into the trap of tailoring their campaigns not to the market, but rather to internal requirements and wishes.

This is how marketing used to work at one of my former employers: the corporate headquarters gave us campaigns that we had to localize for our region. We in marketing thought that we were really good at it, but as soon as we presented our results to the local marketing team, our failure was obvious. The sales team wasn't just skeptical, but they were also really upset with us at times. "Marketing is trying once more to explain to us how the customer ticks, but in reality, they have no idea how the world outside really looks", said one sales colleague after the failed presentation.

The conflict was created because we did not exchange enough information: in time, the marketing team (at headquarters and regionally) had developed their own interpretation of the market. Because marketing and sales failed to connect, the campaigns were simply missing the customer's needs.

Our way of solving that problem began with a new definition of the goals. Every marketing manager had to complete three customer visits per quarter, or, to be more precise, accompany sales on their customer visits. So there was enough opportunity to pick up customer feedback on planned campaigns. In addition, we experienced how our sales colleagues presented to the customers, found out that they don't communicate the correct messaging as often as we wished, and instead modified the messaging that marketing developed, because they thought the content wouldn't appeal to the customer or would be misunderstood.

We improved our understanding rapidly of which news would work for the customers and which wouldn't. We soon realized that not just our marketing messaging, but also our sales enablement tools, were too complicated and too extensive. So we trimmed them down and made them simpler. We were also showing the sales team that we now had direct contact to the customer and took the opportunity to ask marketing questions in order to develop more successful projects in the end. These are also great opportunities for marketers to win the customer as a reference or use them as a speaker in the future.

> **Five Professional Tips to Become a Marketing Business Advisor in Your Company**
> - Take part in the sales team meetings to understand which challenges your colleagues in sales are facing
> - Conceptualize strategic projects that allow you to achieve your goals together quickly and more efficiently. Measure the input of the marketing team by achieving the goal
> - Try to take part in executive meetings within your company because marketing is a strategic investment for every company. Therefore, marketing must influence the strategic planning of your company
> - Communicate the goals that you have achieved, showing the influence of marketing on the success of the business — and do this regularly
> - Communicate facts, facts, facts! (use words like "more", "bigger", and "many")

Six Tips for an Informative Customer Discussion
- In a talk with the customer, center it around the customer: Inquire about the status of a current cooperation, the progress of a certain project or the revenue that your company's products are bringing in. Ask your customer for feedback — what satisfies him, and what doesn't?
- Try to find out what type of a person your contact person is. If he is success-oriented or goal-driven, he might be open to give a reference in the right light. Here is your chance, you grab a good reference for your company
- Ask your customer what his opinion is on a premature campaign from your company. How did he like it? What could he relate to, what not?
- If you are planning an event and you think it might be interesting for this customer, invite them personally
- Make a future appointment at the end of every meeting
- Build up a good relationship with a few select customers, so that you can use their feedback on a campaign or a launch in the future.

"Full Speed Ahead to Real Success"

By Sonja Sulzmaier

"Alignment" is a term from biology and describes behavior that is found in nature in groups of animals. It states that an individual's movement is oriented around their neighbor's. This is a phenomenon, for example, when a group is able to react quickly and compactly against an enemy or intruder, and it is all based on the individual's alignment behavior. Every individual reacts to the behavior of their neighbor. Therefore, a large school of herring is able to make complex movements as one to divert the dolphins and killer whales that try to attack it. Their alignment increases the probability that each individual herring can survive the attack. To do this, each fish must simply concentrate on the movement of a particular amount of their neighbors. The group, however, takes on many individuals in order to react to environmental threats and enable a quick reaction from the group as one unit.

Alignment also means coordinating the direction of movement – a requirement that the herring seem to have perfected, but is difficult in many companies, because the key players may have different goals and ways of assessing success. The same in marketing, product marketing, and sales: Marketing takes a look at the wide range of products and services in the portfolio of the company and orientates themselves around middle to long term goals. Product marketing approaches projects one by one, or on an individual customer basis. Sales is mostly focused on their monthly incoming orders, mainly to measure income, which they seem to concentrate on more than the strategic direction and impact. Therefore, it is no wonder why marketing and sales activities may fail to align in IT companies.

However, in order to ensure that the entire potential of the activities is reached, marketing, product marketing, and sales need to align their roles. In the worst case scenario, activities from marketing and sales can work against each other. An example of this would be brand communication. Only if the sales team actively works as a messenger, and positions the brand positively with the customer, can marketing really be successful. Only when marketing listens to sales in regards to how the customer ticks, can the message of the campaign be driven properly. Marketing is dependent upon their sales colleagues for the formulation of messaging for the customer segments and for the expansion of the campaigns. If this doesn't work and the sales team delivers different messaging to the customer, the brand can become diluted, and the brand's authenticity may be damaged.

Likewise, sales is dependent upon marketing. Let's stick with the brand communication example. This offers orientation and differentiation potential in comparison with other competitors, is also a door opener to customers, and the sales employees are supported with specific messaging for their target customer.

Which methods can you embrace to improve the alignment between marketing and sales? Answers to this question can be found in the following eight core requirements for alignment as well as practice tops for successful implementation.

■ Synchronize Continuously

In order for alignment to function properly, an ongoing exchange between sales and marketing is required. How can this exchange be configured in practice? The first essential step is a common go-to-market plan that defines goals, marketing segments, and service portfolios,

Alignment increases the probability of survival

as well as segment-specific sales and marketing activities and a mandatory time frame for all of the activities. For when marketing and sales activities are not coordinately timed with each other, then it can be that a lot of engagement leads to nothing. A continuous comparison of current strategic points is also constructive to alignment in addition to a go-to-market plan. In order to do this, marketing must participate in sales meetings. Every sales meeting offers new ideas for how the marketing team can support their sales colleagues and vice-versa. Marketing can, for example, present important information to their sales and product marketing colleagues by showing important market analysis, current trends, or a screening of relevant media. At these regularly occurring meetings, marketing can also introduce their goals, activities and campaigns and secure early involvement from sales. It can also be useful to create a common platform for regular exchange of information. And this goes much further than just a mutual Customer Relationship Management System (CRM System). The use of corporate platforms and market monitoring platforms can be two examples of forging alignment so that marketing and sales engage themselves as one entity.

▪ Follow Common Business Development Goals

In all of their activities, marketing and sales should keep their company's strategy and business development in the forefront. Perceived conflicts of goals can often be solved by taking a closer look at the company's strategy. Properly balanced score cards can be a valuable support here. Business development should be one of the most important tasks of both marketing and sales, for here is where markets and service portfolios are analyzed, new businesses are initiated and new business models are drafted.

Involvement in business development can be a deciding factor for the orientation of mutual goals. Sales, who are often concentrated on short term, may lose their orientation of the long term. Marketing, on the other hand, are often not included in the business planning and are often only responsible for creating an appealing and united brand. Marketing and sales involvement in business development is therefore very central, or else there is a risk of driving innovation past the market and customers. Business development is often the missing link that results in the development of collective topics. It can be really useful to anchor marketing organizationally to business development.

In business development, the basic direction is set, upon which everyone should orientate themselves. Everyone must endure the curves and changes in direction that are up ahead.

■ Orientate yourselves around the customer

In addition to the mutual and strategic direction in business development, the market and customer orientation is another important requirement that must be addressed if sales and marketing want to achieve alignment. Since sales are very close to the individual customer, they can bring much useful information to the planning and execution of marketing activities. However, marketing can implement not just the respective market analysis, but they also have the important function of helping sales with an explanation of segment-specific behavior in the field / market. A well-functioning CRM system can deliver clues to the market segmentation and are a useful source of information for each customer relationship. Particularly in IT companies that are product orientated, the CRM system can expose which sales and marketing methods are successful and which activities do not work well. A common evaluation is one of the obligatory tasks of a successful alignment.

In addition to the above, direct contact to the customer is a must for marketing. This contact should not just take place at conventions and events, but should also consist of regular meetings with key customers. There are many topics for discussion: this enables the customer to actually become involved in the marketing development process, depending on their level of satisfaction and plans for the future. There are additional ways to connect with your customers like cooperating together on marketing and PR activities, participating in competitions, and creating presentations for important conferences. Through these activities, marketing can really get a look into the world of the customer and can bring in more value to the customer relationship, creating a competitive advantage.

■ Customize

The sales approach is mostly product specific or customer segmented and in an IT environment, they are often oriented around a single project. The perspective of marketing spans many projects and has the entire message in its view. So that sales employees understand the activities planned by marketing and to ensure their direct implementation, *the customization of activities based on customer segments and products* is a requirement for successful alignment. There will be increased understanding and the support and service that marketing can deliver will be transparent.

Furthermore, there are activities that lie right on the point of intersection between marketing and sales. Here, it pays to conduct direct marketing activities. Customer segment specific direct marketing campaigns will be perceived as important support for the sales team. When you have had your first successful experience, that allows you to generate a mailing or emailing project also in a business to business environment, then it would be unintelligent not to use this opportunity. In this setting, there are correlative CRM systems that facilitate a segment specific, individual approach that is essential.

■ Offer service, service and service!

The service orientation of marketing is one of the most fundamental tools for the acceptance of strategic and operative marketing in the company. As a rule, any advertising campaign will be unsuccessful unless the sales department stands behind it.

Service, service, and service – what can that mean? This actually depends on the daily business of sales, which can vary greatly. This can include requests for proposals, direct marketing campaigns, participation in conventions, creating offers, and presentations at customers. Here, for example, marketing can provide a uniformed tool box of all of the offerings and this can save the sales employees a lot of time. These boxes may contain references for projects in many languages, standard literature about the company and its departments, and product information in multiple languages. In some companies, marketing is used as service for collecting service proposals from other companies; this shows that marketing always has their finger on the trigger. An important component of this tool box can be a concisely constructed presentation template that sales can use to create professional presentations in a short amount of time while knowing that the presentation fulfills any corporate requirements or restrictions.

■ KISS: Keep It Simple and Self-explanatory

The KISS formula is becoming an essential part of the recipe for success – and in many ways. If marketing activities can lead to easing the work flow of sales, they will be immediately accepted and implemented. We can also use the example from above. A simple, uniform presentation template can make the work of sales employees much easier and therefore they accept this gratefully.

In addition, you should keep in mind the KISS formula in regards to marketing communication as well. Simple messages that are immediately understood are easy to deliver and are more accepted and passed along with less error. The customer then receives the proper message.

■ Capitalize on Sales Activities

"The attention of other people is the most irresistible drug." Marketing in IT companies can take this saying to heart. This can also support sales colleagues to capitalize internally and externally on sales success and help them leverage the attention on topics and people. If you offer to help a sales colleague capitalize on their own success, he will not say no to you. In addition to the internal communication of results, you can also help sales capitalize on events, PR activities, (interviews, press conferences, customer magazines) and the organization of presentation opportunities at important conferences. Particularly excellent projects and activities may qualify to participate in competitions with a good reputation. Whoever wins a prize or an honor also earns the bonus of attention, which leads to new motivation.

■ Measure Success

It is obvious that an evaluation of success is necessary. The definition and inquiry of useful measures of success is central to the alignment of marketing and sales. Unfortunately, the use of marketing's work and their effect on the company's success is not (or only partly) able to be quantified, while the primary measure of success for sales is simply the ability to bring in revenue. Here, it is necessary to generate corresponding reporting options that also contain means of measuring quality. Balanced scorecards can also be applied here. In addition to the adherence of goals and the given budgets, possible measurements of success could be the number of generated leads, the conversion of these leads into prospects (more specifically into customers), the response to specific campaigns and events, customer satisfaction, or the level of the company's brand recognition in specific markets. Online marketing activities can be immediately measured (users reached, click through rates, conversions, etc.). Of course, the measurements of success should also be correlated with a competitive perspective, through respective benchmarks and direct comparison. Online platforms offer a comparison of press clippings which can present the exact number of times a competitor was mentioned in the press.

The rating of activities, including CRM, will often conclude that the cooperation between sales and marketing when addressing current or future customers is the key to success for customer acquisition and relationships.

■ The Bottom Line

When marketing and sales stay on the same page, they will have way more success together than they could have alone. Just like the school of fish, in a business context, teams that are well aligned will experience more movement than even the exceptional individual, who has a different strategy. Stepping out of the line can be full of risk and should only occur in certain situations. The method of aligning sales and marketing for activities in both departments is the only way to have the full power of their capabilities. Through use of the eight key requirements above, marketing and sales activities will not just experience increased effectiveness, but they will also be able to react quicker together to any changes in their environment. In addition, the understanding and acceptance of marketing activities will improve within the company.

Beating your Own Drum
How you can capitalize on your work

"Do something good and then talk about it"- this isn't just true for the company and their products, services, or solutions; this is also true for marketing itself. A marketer must market themselves and their work, and then lastly they will need a budget and good employees to reach their goals. And he will only receive both of these when the key decision makers know what role marketing plays in the fulfillment of the company's goals. Therefore, you have to tell them – and tell them often. Then, they will understand that good marketing requires sustainability. Only when a recipient hears the message five to seven times, will it sink in. Their time and endurance is tested, even though they will find it better, to invest their time directly in marketing projects.

You can approach "Marketing for marketing" very differently, like when you are proving what marketing does for the company as a whole. For example, how you approach an external imaging campaign one way, and then how you would marketing individual products another way, you should first initiate a permanent internal image campaign and then advertise with specifically targeted projects.

With almost every approach, an internal imaging campaign takes place – in individual discussions, in meetings or in presentations, via email or the company intranet. In short, your image campaign should be based on a mix of communication channels and situations in which different levels of details are present – three PowerPoint slides on current project successes, an email about the achievements of the marketing team, a monthly newsletter to all colleagues in which you inform them about the current and future projects planned. You should invest time and effort into this and formulate stringent messaging. This should not be some passing task, as this is a

> "Personal success is not a question of who has the best ideas, but rather the result of an impressive presentation of these ideas, and therefore – the individual person." –
> EMIL HIERHOLD

real part of your work, and above all, you should prepare your arguments with cold hard facts that no one can ignore.

For some marketers, self-marketing is in their blood. Capitalizing on their own person and their own talents comes naturally for them. Some can do this with charm and without being pretentious; others can get on your nerves. If you don't fall into either of these categories, don't worry – you have good company. In this case, just follow the classic saying: Only a few have the talent, but many can learn it. You just have to want it.

I personally spent years learning presentation and rhetoric techniques in training and I presented for a few years myself until I really felt comfortable (although I still feel nervous from time to time). I always recommend that people who do not feel confident about presenting should attend similar trainings. Developing a concept for internal marketing in which you can formulate your messaging and work out your campaigns (like you are used to doing as a marketer) is just as important as presenting it. Finally, you will need endurance as well as moderation.

Crisis PR on Your Own Account

It is nice to market your own success. Although it is not as nice, it is just as important to communicate bad news timely and openly such as a project that didn't deliver the desired results or the correction of a campaign that did not have the right resonance on the market. The time-sensitive deliverance of bad news is important because it will make you believable because you are transparent in your communication.

I, therefore, announce negative news proactively, even when I might have to dig myself out of a hole. Hiding the mistake and believing that no one will find out doesn't work. Good management requires open communication and acting on the offense, even if things aren't going so well, because you only have one chance to present the news yourself and eventually put a positive spin on it – like the following example shows:

For the launch of a new software solution, we developed an elaborate campaign. The product seemed really complex to us in marketing, so we thought, it is only possible to communicate this in five coordinated steps. We presented the concept to sales, who dissected it piece by piece. "Too boring and way too complicated", they said. Then they recommended that we take the concept down to three steps, but we knew better in marketing, and we engaged ourselves for weeks in that project.

When we executed a customer test before the actual publication of the campaign, from which we expected to receive confirmation and encouragement, we learned something even better. The customers also found our messaging to be too complicated and the campaign to be too pompous, exactly like the sales colleagues suspected. We in marketing had to modify the campaign and notify management as well as sales. It was so pointless that during the initial discussions, we had argued so vehemently for the five complicated steps. Afterwards, we communicated our error and the required modifications proactively: we thanked the sales team for their critique and presented the customer test results, along with a new follow up campaign that we were able to finance with the savings. Sales was satisfied, and the customer feedback was absolutely positive.

Persuasion with Structure

The more innovative the idea, the better the presentation has to be prepared. It is especially important to plan for the thoughts and opinions of your managers and colleagues so that you are able to rebut their possible objections. In order for this to succeed, you should prepare yourself for criticism, even though you may be really excited for the project. Where are the weak areas and what are the risks? How can we minimize these risks? What is plan B when this project doesn't work?

Hold the presentation or discussion with many people and it is helpful to introduce the project in advance to several people who will actually participate. This will help you to gather some possible feedback and identify possible weak points so that you can arm yourself correspondingly.

This rule is true for every presentation and discussion: you have to get your audience to nod. The earlier and the more fervently they nod, the better. So it would be ideal to begin with something that everyone can nod to. Something like: "In the upcoming year, we would like to increase our market share of red gummy bears by 20%". If this is the one constant of the business strategy that everyone can relate to, they will nod.

Wonderful. This is a great beginning that can lead up the presentation of your new project ideas. The trick is to present a high level goal to the audience, like a revenue target for the entire company or a new target market. It can give you an advantage if you present in the beginning exactly what value the company would gain from your project or a nice way to awaken interest. As soon as the attention is turned to you, refer to your project, the strategy behind it, how you plan to address the target group, the means, and relevant figures.

The type of presentation should be tailored to your audience. You can present orally or with help from a PowerPoint presentation in a management meeting. It is important that your messaging is stringent and you must repeat it often. The argument that you have already presented your plan in departmental meetings is invalid. As long as there are colleagues in the meeting who are not yet informed, you must repeat your argument. It is vital that you tailor your content to your audience – the management should get an executive overview, while the marketing managers receive the juicy details.

Another example, if you are a marketing manager at a smaller, less well-known company and you want to present an innovative idea, you can begin with the following: "I was contemplating how we can secure the most attention possible in our market, with very little resources. With this idea, we can substantially increase our recognition, which our sales colleagues will really enjoy."

You then begin with positive results, the advantage, the actual value. Everyone will nod. Alternatively, you could begin with a rhetorical question like "Isn't our mutual goal to increase the level of brand recognition for our company?" or "Don't we all want to give sales easy access to the customer?" These types of questions can only be answered with "yes", and these yes's pave the way for agreement with your proposal later. Just use sayings like "If we all agree to this in the beginning..." or "So it is all in our best interest..."

Many presenters make the mistake of doing the exact opposite. They begin with discussing their project in detail and then move on to presenting the actual benefit to everyone. The problem with this way of presenting is that the audience cannot understand the context correctly if they are listening to many project details. Because they are not able to identify what the real aim of the project is, they might develop a negative impression of the project or become bored.

If you begin with the real value that this brings to the company and its employees – demonstrated above – it is recognizable that you are on the right path strategically. Your project's success is the success of the company, and therefore the success of your manager. As soon as the audience understands this concept, your project is approved.

In our small, less-known example company, people will also agree to do something to increase the recognition of the company. After you have gotten a few nods or positive murmurs from them, begin explaining the details of your project:

"In order to increase our company's recognition on the market, we have to do things that our industry has never seen before. Then, we will have a surprise effect on the market without spending lots of money on an image campaign."

You have just revealed an important first part of your idea. You want to do something new and extraordinary. Everyone will also agree with you here, because doing something to increase the company's image with little cost is always attractive.

Maybe someone asks: "Yeah, and how is that going to work?" but, even if the audience is formulating critical questions, it shows that they are curious and are interested. Still continue to present the details of your project.

Don't be mistaken and think that now your work is done and you will receive unlimited approval. Normally, there will be a round of critical questions and then suddenly your project has a managing committee. A possible defense against this could be: "You have forgotten that we have such a small company and if we proceed this way, our budget will not even cover the catering. I think we need to take a couple steps back and park that idea for a few years."

When you face tough criticism in that direction, you can always refer back to the constant target. "Also an idea, but with that idea we won't change anything. Sales could work noticeably easier and faster if the customer knew our company and sales wouldn't have to explain who we are and what we do every time. With the massive press coverage from this event alone, we will substantially increase our company's recognition."

At the end, you can present your cost plans and details about the risk the company is taking on. That is an additional important part of your presentation. It's all about the costs and risks that your manager must take on. Because risk always exists, it is good to refer to the opportunities once more at this point, and you should emphasize what the company stands to lose if they do not follow through with this project. Clearly restate how fantastic it would be to increase the brand recognition and product image of your company.

Flame Throwers

Whether it's good news or bad news, it doesn't matter. What you communicate must be authentic if you want to impress others. Therefore, try to be the professional that you are with regards to your feelings about professional issues. If you are excited about a project, you should make it noticeable, and also vice-versa, if you are upset about a project that has gone downhill, you don't have to conceal your disappointment. If you are a more serious person, try to lighten up your presentation with a few jokes and word-plays. It may work really will with the audience.

You should never forget that enthusiasm is the most important aspect of your presentation – it is contagious. The more you burn for your project, the more you will inspire the others to come on board with you, even if the topic is new to your audience.

During a normal work day that pulls you here and there, how can you keep your motivation up? This is a question that many other books address. Here I can just give you one tip – take care of your self-motivation like your brush your teeth every day. Do whatever motivates you consciously and create time for it each day. Imagine what success you could achieve and which interesting tasks you could take on, etc. Then, your excitement and motivation will be awakened.

"Being successful requires two things- clear goals and the burning desire to achieve them." – JOHANN WOLFGANG GOETHE

Marketing through Listening

A fatal flaw of marketing is speaking too much and not listening enough. Don't make this mistake. Whoever is giving a monologue is getting nothing in return from his counterpart.

Of course, it is necessary to communicate your point clearly, but the ideas and opinions of your audience are then lost. The golden rule that I always train myself with is listen closely first and then give your own opinion. Sometimes I have even discarded my own perceptions because the other side of things seemed better to me, or maybe there were new aspects that I had not thought of yet – and I still have to look for the answers.

Critical Colleagues

> "Nothing ruins more than the three words: that won't work. Whenever I hear that, I do anything to make the impossible possible." –
> HARALD ZINDLER

Unfortunately, almost every group dynamic has someone who will do his best to change the positive atmosphere of the group. In order to avoid this, it is important to look your critical colleagues in the eyes and communicate very clearly with them. Many make the mistake of not interacting with critical colleagues. This is a strategy that can do downhill very quickly. Then the critic has the opportunity to act without restrictions and they can become a trouble maker. Therefore, it is important to take the wind out of the critics by positioning yourself very clearly from the beginning.

Try to speak with your critical colleagues, or else you run the risk of these feelings building up in the critic and then you are confronted with topics or emotions that are now out of control, or even worse: the critic becomes popular and builds up a wall against you.

Present what you can do right in front of the complainer, for it is hard to ignore evident success. An especially effective method of communicating with critics is to include them in your projects. Therefore, I invite Mr. Grumpy and Co. directly to our meetings and discussions. So I then get the chance to hear other points of criticism. Sometimes, one of these critics can bring a good point to the table. It would be even more intelligent to thank these people for their valuable input. Smaller, less potent arguments will simply disappear.

My experience is that critics are mostly developed because

the critic does not know all of the aspects of the project or maybe they misunderstood something. Once these questions are answered, the problem may be solved due to open communication and listening.

If this doesn't end positively, perhaps a marketing campaign can help, in which the critic profits. At my old employer, we had a large sales team and all-in-all, we cooperated very well together, except for in this team, there was a special group for finance and we could not get on a productive, cooperating level with them. No matter what we did, they viewed us badly – as a burden, bringing nothing to the company. Through the course of time, this attitude manifested and after a row of discussions, it could not be tamed.

We needed concrete success to show that we actually brought value to the company. We wanted to achieve this with targeted Named Account Marketing, so we developed a strategic marketing plan for a customer, to make them trust us with our products and solutions. This approach was new to sales. We were able to generate some curiosity, at least. Suddenly, we experienced success. Even after the first presentation, the customer wanted more. We developed an entire series out of it, and in a short amount of time, sales had a huge amount of newly interested customers from other companies.

Of course, word got around the sales team, and then every sales manager wanted similar events for their key accounts. This didn't just create a better relationship with Finance, but after one year, we were able to hire someone just for Key Accounts Management – and this was one of our key project goals.

> "In a discussion, the most important part is what is not being said." –
> PETER F. DRUCKER

Seven Tips for Self-Marketing

- Do good and talk about it – internally too! If you experience success, you should communicate it
- Excite yourself with your ideas. As soon as you burn for your idea, your audience will too
- Facts, facts, facts – this is what your work and your self-marketing is based on. Set facts in place with regards to the entire company's success; benchmarks that compare your progress with your industry
- Be brave and take risks. You will make your mark and not just your project will be perceived differently, you will too!
- Always begin your argument with what use your project can bring – what marketing can bring the entire company, for marketing serves a purpose for the company
- Listen to what the others want and compare this with your goals and project ideas. What works? What doesn't work (yet)?
- Stay in touch with your critics: Embrace their arguments and address the substantial points – and rebuff those complainers.

"Fire and Flame for Innovation"

By Guido Happe

In this article, you should receive a quick overview of the factors that create the foundation of innovation. To enable a foundation, here, means the excitement and enthusiasm of management for innovation, as well as the necessity of the business culture and top management to recognize this.

The wish for structure and innovation, or even reform, is not what is important here, but rather the current reality and the existing ground work.

Innovation is simply some materialistic or symbolic artifacts, which the audience perceives as new and an improvement in comparison with whatever existed before that.

Six types of innovation can be identified and defined:

- Product Innovation
  Product innovation is new or improved products. The primary factor here is the buyer's decision and use over the already existing products

- Process Innovation
  This innovation brings new aspects to the services of an existing company. Process innovations are, for example, the increase in security aspects or an increase in productivity

- Market-type Innovation
  With this type of innovation, new markets and acquisitions are targeted. For example, new vendor or customer groups, in order to achieve more revenue,

or, on the other side, to decrease costs or to improve the quality of products or services

- Structural Innovation
  Structural innovations are, for example, reformations or new directions in the work structure. This could be something like the implementation of a new work model, new tactics, or personal development, a new sales model or go-to-market model – like franchising

- Cross-Industry Innovation
  Here, technologies, knowledge, and resources from different industries are integrated into the work process of a company, in order to support cooperation from all sides and to promote new developments. An example of this would be the use of technological developments from space travel in the automobile industry.

- Intermittent Innovation = Revolution
  This type of innovation is surely the most meaningful, because revolutional thinking always leads to change

These different types of innovation make it absolutely clear which required aspects must already be in place. Top management and employees must prepare, present, and decide on their professional vision and spirit, to various degrees. Innovation is more like maneuverable coincidences that require someone close to reality to think outside of the box.

What constitutes an Innovation?
- Innovation should absolutely positively increase revenue. A stark look at cost optimization and process optimization doesn't always cut it.

- Innovation has to create something new or a leap (either forward or ahead of the competition)
- It has to be well thought out, what the influence could or will be on the entire organization (this is risk minimization). For the release of budgets, personal resources, and the implementation of ideas are always an emotional vs. experience decision. That means you should make your decision livable. Less is more: concrete, clear, and efficiently communicated
- If the technical part of the innovation is emphasized the most, this doesn't always suffice. In the B2B area, the innovation has to generate a brand effect, a charisma – in order to create a mandatory provision (Customer Experience).
- The innovation team has to position themselves enthusiastically and passionately, but at the same time, they have to make it clear that they are unbiased and are in the position to question all ideas free from politics and personal preferences.
- Cost optimization and minimization should be viewed better as a project. The development of new markets and revenue as well as intermittent innovation, aka revolution, are not projects in the sense – innovation finds an audience, projects less so.

What do employees have to bring to the table in order to impress top management?

- The ability to calculate failure – planning the business to the very end
- The ability to decide
- Endurance and dependability
- Strength in communication

- The ability to create demand and fulfill demand
- Realistic self-confidence and the ability to accept criticism
- Flexibility in constantly changing situations

What does a company and those in top management have to offer structurally and culturally, in order to see, sense, understand, and implement innovation?

- Imagination (Many top managers are hindered because they can't imagine anything new)
- Freedom to think
- The ability to lead the team through good and bad
- The ability to allow free space and the ability to accept mistakes – not just accept, but encourage them in order to learn!
- The revolutionary passion for change and anything new

The most innovative company can demonstrate this through Customer Experience, through the ability to turn over every stone and through this, bring new, successful products on to the market. Culturally, the most innovative companies also show bravery when it comes to decision making, is an impressive and desirable necessity, even above experience. This courage leads to the creation of more professional processes and strong products.

A company can only develop further if they question themselves.

For example, the top three most innovative companies recognize the patterns. These patterns can and must be used by the employees, in order to bring a movement for change into the benchmark perspective of top management, and therefore they can use the chance to compare rather than mirror. For being present is everything, there is much more happening when you are there.

The top three most innovative companies, according to "BusinessWeek" and the Boston Consulting Company, are Apple, Google, and General Electric (and out of the top 100 companies that made the *Forbes List* in 1917, only one remains there today – and that is General Electric).

Innovational patterns (the criteria to make it to the top and stay there) are:

- The so-called Customer Experience at Apple, which is their intuition for sexy product designs, effective marketing, and their creation of undeniably amazing products.

- The product diversity at Google, their creation of their customer experience, the ability to discover new things and make them available, the high speed of decision making and their corporate culture which is built on constant change.

- At General Electric, it would be their exemplary process work, new way of managing, and their leading efficiency. GE has a reputation for thinking new products through and executing securely through their top internal processes.

We can see in this short passage how complex the requirements on managers and employees are, to not just live the innovation, but to completely care for their innovational abilities. Bes practices are an intelligent means, but courage and passion are the real deciding factors – and you must deliver this yourself and demand it from your colleagues.

The Numbers Have to be There

Here's how your marketing can be measurably more effective:

Whoever wants to be viewed as a solid marketing manager has to work with numbers – even if this isn't usually in the blood of marketers. This is not just about your task of working with budget figures, which is always required of marketers. It is just especially important to show your success in numbers. This is about showing concrete results from marketing campaigns: How many downloads? How many calls? How many orders? This is also about consolidated numbers: How many leads did marketing generate? How many concrete sales opportunities? How much revenue?

Accordingly, the marketing director must also control the tool of success measurement, just like the sales director or the CEO uses the revenue figures to map out goals and underpin success. Slowly, it is becoming unacceptable to simply say that a marketing campaign was successful. Instead, hard facts have to be on the table. In this instance, it is not just important to follow the KPIs (Key Performance Indicators) in order to measure success, it is important to define the goals with KPIs in advance.

It's in the boss' best interest...

Thanks to investor relations, the key figures of a company are transparent nowadays. You know which company yields how much revenue (and sometimes you even wonder why they let some employees go). Everyone knows the earnings per share of different cost ratios. You can even find the remuneration of an executive board, if you are familiar with a German stock corporation's annual report. Also, in terms of transparency in marketing and the demands that the corporation puts on its marketers, many companies already have a marketing measurement in place.

It's best if everyone monitors themselves

It's as true in marketing as it is in accounting: Numbers are only a useful management tool when they are correct and complete. There are a variety of tools that you can use for this – above all, a well maintained database. Ideally, the whole corporation has a CRM system, which grants all of the staff quick access to the same records. In reality, many companies are missing the right tool and departments manage with Excel spreadsheets, where the data is neither complete, nor recorded promptly.

Just as important as a CRM tool is an online marketing analysis program. This not only inspects the visitor activities on the website, but also handles the email campaigns via the website. Then, whoever is associated with each campaign on the site can not only act and inform especially quickly, but also measure the resonance of the customer. In short, using the online analysis software can be a direct influence on proving the marketing success on the sales pipeline. This is an important aspect when it comes to acquiring more budgets internally. Whoever wants to have the best overview of the whole lot of data uses a marketing dashboard, where the touch of a button shows how much budget is in which product groups, markets and target flows. Ideally, any marketing staff controls the means of measuring marketing effectiveness themselves and uses the information as necessary to promptly respond when the numbers evolve differently than they expect.

Should the figures in the interim analysis suggest that you missed the marketing objectives, you put counter measures into place in time. Also, you can produce positive developments immediately – if targets are exceeded because the market responds surprisingly well on a campaign, the mar-

> "Measure everything that can be measured, and make everything measurable which is not." – GALILEO GALILEI

keter has two choices: He can make the maximum use of the positive trend or he can settle with the current achievements and then let the remaining budget flow to another campaign. That is, the evaluations help the responsible managers measure short-term results and distribute resources optimally.

Budgeting with Indicators – and Intuition

In times of crisis – and afterwards – budgeting in marketing resembles the quadrature of the circle. The budgets are smaller, but the effect achieved is expected to be larger. How to distribute the budget the best? What can we do without this? What you absolutely need? My opinion is that at the worst times, you can save on everything except public relations, for the first impression of us as a company is the written word we use and good PR material can be used in many different ways. You can use existing text for the company website, individual text components can be used in mailing campaigns and so on and so on. This multiple use is intelligent and it's efficient.

Just as important as good public relations is a high quality database, (see above) because it is the essential basis for the metrics-based marketing efforts. The more meaningful the data collected, the better to set up the end campaigns.

Third, you should always have current website content and make this link with the database. With online-efficiency programs, you can evaluate almost every click of a prospect: the success of the website is then measurable and you can draw important conclusions.

If you belong to the group of lucky marketers whose budget is not so exhausted, I also recommend investing in strategic, sequential -building campaigns. However, planning security for several quarters is risky because if such a campaign must be stopped halfway instead of running its length, the campaign may simply waste money and resources.

Figures are not only relevant for the control of individual

projects, but they also provide the basis for the annual or quarterly total budget planning. Experience from previous quarters or year can show which results were achieved by which measures. This is then useful for estimating what the marketing mix should be for the desired results. Or the other way around: is the objective clear? Such as the opening of new markets, the launch of specific products or sales targets? In general, can we determine which key projects are required in order to achieve the objectives? But key figures alone cannot determine the marketing mix. In addition, you need a dose of intuition. In all calculations, evaluations and analysis, only the final personal assessment of budget decisions makes it perfect.

"To us in the endless stream of personal decisions that we always have to make, in order to find your way, it is crucial to feel." –

DANIEL GOLEMAN

"Nothing is Created Through Pure Thinking"

By Neil Morgan

"Half of my marketing expenditure is a mere waste," complained John Wanamaker, the owner of the American department store, Wanamaker's. "Unfortunately I do not know which half." This statement from the 19th century has lost none of its validity even in the 21st century.

The desire to really understand the effectiveness of targeted marketing investments has achieved the status of a "Holy Grail" almost, which we have accepted in the past. This has inevitably led to the conclusion that the days of obscure marketing activities – one based on gut feeling and instinct – are over. The key to this change lies in the rapid rise of digital marketing.

Finally the opaque days of marketing are over. Period.

The rise of digital marketing from 1-2 % of total spend a decade ago to anything form 25-100 % of campaign spend in major organsiations today has changed forever the expectations of marketers in the way they measure what they do.

Marketers in the past decade have seen how effective it is to use digital channels with budget flowing to tools like search marketing, online advertising, affiliate marketing and more recently social marketing. Apart from its effectiveness, it is because it is so measurable, that digital has grown so much in recent years,. It has allowed marketers to stand up and be counted, in many cases becoming accountable for their actions in ways never before seen.

As marketers, we should be concerned about our marketing investments, but more importantly, our jobs! This challenge also underscores the love/hate relationship that frequently exists between marketing and sales organizations. Sales teams complain that marketing doesn't generate enough leads to get the sales cycle moving or that marketing's activities aren't meeting their intended goals. Marketing complains that if the sales team were producing more sales, then marketing would have more budget to do the marketing activities that would produce more meaningful leads.

There's an overriding question that marketers and sales organizations should ask themselves though: Are leads really the end game? What about the number of meaningful sales opportunities per month? The number of net new customers gained? Or a campaign's overall return on investment? When used properly, analytics can create marketing nirvana for marketers because they can know the exact answers to all of the above questions. Marketers can easily understand what's working and what isn't. They can better allocate marketing budget toward those activities that are most effective at achieving their key performance indictors and eliminate those that aren't producing.

A simple, recent example illustrates how lead generation vs. conversions from leads-to-sales made a big difference in the marketing and demand generation efforts here at Omniture, An Adobe company. Recently, our marketing team promoted both a free webinar and a downloadable guide on the topic of "8 Critical Success Factors for Lead Generation. So which one, the guide or webinar, performed the best? This is a misleading question because the follow up question from the person being asked should be, "Performed the best based on which metric? Leads, sales opportunities, closed deals, close rate, etc."

Here are the answers: The downloadable guide converted 42 % more leads than the webinar. At the outset, you would think the company would have emphasized and promoted the guide over the webinar, however, you would have guessed wrong. It turns out that even though the webinar generated fewer leads, it was 155 % better at converting those leads to sales-ready opportunities and had an 80 % better close ratio from sales opportunity to closed deal. Now don't run out and stop the presses on white papers and guides in favor of webinars just because of this test. In speaking with Tony Jaros of Sirius Decisions, a Sales and Marketing effectiveness research firm, his advice is that the topic is the area that drives the most effectiveness and where it fits into the buying cycle, not so much about whether it was a webinar or white paper format; we're going to test another version by promoting both together and look deeper at the results which was his advice.

Gaining this kind of information was made possible by integrating Omniture's Web analytics applications with its CRM system – becoming more than Web analytics, but full marketing analytics capable of measuring off- and online events including tradeshow performance, direct mail, as well as offline sales pipeline metrics. For Omniture, integrating analytics with a our CRM system, as you would imagine, is an important step to tying the entire lead generation and sales process together and measuring the combined process. We've found three key benefits to doing so:

- Better marketing investment prioritization (for both time and money)
- Measure marketing's contribution to the sales pipeline
- Enable sales intelligence for improved selling context

Real Metrics & KPIs for B2B Marketing

Businesses and their marketing organizations that promote products or services with complex sales cycles often lack visibility beyond generating the initial sales leads from their Web sites, trade shows or other offline initiatives. For example, once Web leads are generated, they move into the black hole of the SFA/CRM system with almost no ability to tie results such as closed deal quantities and sales values back to the marketing campaign costs, thus leaving fully measured ROI (or return on marketing) unanswered. To provide concrete answers to these ROI and other related questions, marketers should endeavor to integrate their Web analytics/campaign management solutions together with their SFA/CRM applications. In lieu of this type of integration, most marketers are confined to measuring premature and often, misleading campaign metrics such as total lead quantities and their associated cost-per-lead metrics as a basis for performance. Once marketers are enabled to measure metrics beyond initial lead conversion such as:

- Qualified leads and sales opportunities
- Closed deals
- Sales values

all at a campaign or tracking code level, marketers can prioritize which marketing investments such as advertising placements (which keywords, banner ad placements, email, etc.), site promotions (webinars, white papers, product tours, etc.) are yielding results deeper in the sales cycle relative to their counterparts. Derivative metrics such as creating Sales, Cost, and Customer per

- Impression
- Click/Event Conversation

- Lead
- Qualified Lead / Sales-Ready Leads / Opportunities
- Customer

can provide meaningful insight into the effectiveness at every stage in the marketing and sales cycle.

However there are many complexities of measuring marketing to accounts which are most often comprised of multiple contacts or committees, such as in high consideration B2C purchasing or in the complex purchasing cycles of B2B organsiations.

Introducing Marketing Nirvana; Campaign Attribution

Once marketers are enabled to tie campaigns to metrics deeper in the sales cycle such as closed deals, sales values, and sales-ready leads, determining which campaign to associate to the metrics becomes a complicated process. One closed deal could possibly have 10 or more different campaigns associated to it depending on the number of campaigns associated with each contact and the total number of unique contacts (both decision makers and influencers) on the account. To provide a meaningful solution to this problem, marketers should deploy a multi-campaign touch / source methodology and analysis which allows marketers to define multiple ROI campaign views from which to make marketing investment decisions. I recommend at least four different campaign views that are most important and influential to every closed deal:

First source – which campaign / interaction sourced the account (not just the lead) into your database regardless of how long ago it happened.

Marketing touched – that any campaign / interaction

(defined as a meaningful exchange or interaction – i.e. they downloaded a paper, took the product tour, attended an event; companies can decide if they want to include less engaging metrics such as a click to a particular product or personalize landing page or click-through from an email.

Last touch – The interaction just before the opportunity is created. I'm defining sales-ready opportunity as the phone or in-person meeting between a sales professional and prospect to review the solution (once the authority of the prospect and potential need or interest have been established). This last touch (also referred by some, as "progressed" i.e. Sirius Decisions) often demonstrates which interaction is most influential in getting the account to "meet" with you.

Combination of marketing touched – this would be a report that would show you the combination of campaigns / interactions at an account level to show which interactions worked harmoniously to create the opportunity; this could also be created an roll up level to decide which combination of campaigns / interactions were the most common to a grouping of closed deals or created opportunities.

About the Guest Authors of the Passages

Anke Meyer-Grashorn

Anke Meyer-Grashorn studied marketing and in 1996, she founded the company große freitheit LLC, which specializes in topics like innovational culture and open innovation. Today, she is an established innovation consultant and expert on the production of ideas. She is a faculty member at Steinbeis Hochschule in Germany, a well known speaker, and author of two German books – "Spinnen ist Pflicht – Querdenken und Neues schaffen" and "Trust Yourself! Wie Sie ihr Intution für Entscheidungen nutzen". Her customers are Adobe Systems, Bayer CropScience, Bayerischer Runkfunk, BMW Group, DATEV e. V., Postbank Deutschland, Gigaset, Henkel, Raiffeisenbank Wien, Tchibo, Walt Disney Company, and more.

Monika Scheddin

Former top manager Monika Scheddin founded the Woman's Business Academy LLC in 1994, as well as the Woman's Business Club in Frankfurt and Munich, Germany. As an expert in networking, she was a long term lecturer at the Ludwig-Maximilians-University in Munich and she is the initiator of the Good-People Luncheons. Her book, "Erfogsstrategie Networking" is a top seller. (www.Scheddin.com)

Gabriele Rittinghaus

Gabiele Rittinghaus has more than 20 years of experience in sales and general management in the IT industry. Since the beginning of 2009 she has been the managing director of FINAKI Germany, an intermediate company that works between the responsible IT people (CIOs) at the biggest German companies and the vendor companies of the IT and telecommunications industry. In the past, she worked for CA Computer Associates for 14 years, where she was the managing director for the German organization. In addition, she was a CEO for a CRM company as they made their initial public offering.

Torsten Bittlingmaier

Since the middle of 2009, Torsten Bittlingmaier has been leading the corporate talent management at the German headquarters of Telekom. Before this, he was the Vice President of global human resources for the worldwide HR organization at Software AG, and for four years, he was the leader of the personal and organizational development department at MAN Nutzfahrzeuge AG. In the 90's, he was employed in the human resources departments of many prominent German companies.

Sonja Sulzmaier

Sonja Sulzmaier possesses over 10 years of marketing experience in the high tech environment. She is a corporate marketing manager of ESG Electronic Systems and Logistics LLC, one of the leading IT system integration and engineering services companies in Germany, as well as the marketing manager of the sister consulting company of ESG Consulting LLC. Before, she was working for the Boston Consulting Group as a consultant for international projects in the IT, Engineering, and Pharmaceutical fields. She is a faculty professor in Strategy and Online Marketing at the Witten / Herdecke University and the University of the Arts in Berlin. Her final dissertation on airport business redesign was nominated as one of the best of her year in 1999 at the Witten / Herdecke University. She has published many works with topics such as business redesign, strategic marketing, and online marketing.

Guido Happe

Since 2009, Guido Happe has been the head of Steinbach Consulting. He previously worked at Keinbaum Executive Consultants LLC as partner and manager of the Competence Center for Advanced Technologies for about nine years, focusing on national and international executive search projects. As one of the partners at Keinbaum, he was also responsible for venture capital and start up management. Guido Happe is the founder of the advisory panel, www.beiratforum.de and is also an active member of the advisory board of two IT / technology companies. He is an author and editor of different publication from Gabler Publishing House.

Neil Morgan

Neil Morgan is the senior director of Digital Marketing at Adobe Systems for the EMEA Region (Europe, the Middle East and Africa). In his career as executive marketer for enterprise software, he has over 20 years of experience from all different areas of marketing, from product management to product marketing to channel marketing, public relations, and analyst relations. In addition, he uses his position in Europe and internationally to gain wide reaching experience in international business. In the last 10 years, he has worked directly with customers on different CRM or digital marketing systems. Right before he came to Adobe, he was breathing life into the European marketing team at Omniture, which now is a part of Adobe. He was also the leader of the EMEA marketing team at Siebel Systems and he was the vice president for worldwide marketing at Chordiant Software. He also held different international positions at Oracle Corporation, in San Mateo – Oracle's headquarters.